# Student Relevance Matters

# Student Relevance Matters

## Why Do I Have to Know This Stuff?

Mickey Kolis

ROWMAN & LITTLEFIELD EDUCATION

*A division of*

ROWMAN & LITTLEFIELD PUBLISHERS, INC.
*Lanham • New York • Toronto • Plymouth, UK*

Published by Rowman & Littlefield Education
A division of Rowman & Littlefield Publishers, Inc.
A wholly owned subsidiary of The Rowman & Littlefield Publishing Group, Inc.
4501 Forbes Boulevard, Suite 200, Lanham, Maryland 20706
http://www.rowmaneducation.com

Estover Road, Plymouth PL6 7PY, United Kingdom

British Library Cataloguing in Publication Information Available

**Library of Congress Cataloging-in-Publication Data**

Kolis, Mickey, 1954–
  Student relevance matters : why do I have to know this stuff? / Mickey Kolis.
    p. cm.
  Includes index.
  ISBN 978-1-60709-915-4 (cloth : alk. paper)—ISBN 978-1-60709-916-1 (pbk. : alk. paper)—ISBN 978-1-60709-917-8 (electronic)
   1. Education—Curricula—United States. 2. Education—Aims and objectives—United States. 3. Educational change—United States. I. Title.
  LB1570.K626  2011
  375.00973—dc22
                                                                                              2010052498

♾ ™ The paper used in this publication meets the minimum requirements of American National Standard for Information Sciences—Permanence of Paper for Printed Library Materials, ANSI/NISO Z39.48-1992.

Printed in the United States of America

# Contents

# Foreword

When I was a new teacher educator, I remember meeting one-on-one with my student teachers every week, going over their lesson plans to give them positive feedback and to make suggestions for improvement. I have a vivid memory of reading one set of plans for a high school social studies teacher and being struck that something was missing in her set of history lessons on the United States in the eighteenth century. Her eyes got very big when I looked up from the plans and said, "You've organized these materials very clearly, but I wonder if you've thought about why students should learn about the Constitutional Convention?"

We had a wonderful talk then about connecting the subject area to its purpose in the lives of learners. I'm pleased to say that, fueled by her love of history as well as her concern for her learners, this student teacher rose to the challenge and, from that day, thought about ways to connect her lessons to her learners' lives, experiences, and questions. But I sometimes wonder if she would have sustained her career as a teacher if she had not confronted the key point in Mickey Kolis's book, how we find deep, meaningful answers to why they have to know this stuff.

The connection between the school subjects and their purposes is even more important today because of the kind of demands our students face as they look to a future in a global economy and multicultural world. The fact-based approach to schooling that Kolis describes—all too familiar to anyone who has spent time in schools across the United States—will not prepare our young people for the kinds of expectations that Tony Wagner (2008) describes as "the new world of work" and others call "twenty-first-century learning" (The Partnership for Twenty-First-Century Skills).

In order to approach problems and challenges as a learner instead of a knower, students need to develop the habit of asking good questions and rekindle their curiosity about why things are the way they are or why some things are important and others not. Just such critical thinking and problem solving can be nurtured when teachers engage learners in exploring ideas and building cognitive skills.

For this new world, our students need to learn to work effectively with others, those who look and/or think like themselves and those who don't. They need to learn to work across boundaries of history and culture, seeking to understand how others have made sense of their lives. A fact-based curriculum doesn't build skills in collaboration, networking, and leadership based in influence and persuasion. While a fact-based school may prepare students for the teacher's quiz, it is sadly lacking when students have to face negotiating their way through critical interactions with others.

Another set of skills highlighted by the Partnership for Twenty-First-Century Skills focuses on communication. It's clearly a skill that was needed in every prior century as well. The difference is that now we expect all learners to leave schools with effective skills in reading, writing, listening, and speaking (Resnick, 2010). The fact-based school does not do a good job of building strong communication skills for all.

What today's learners need and can find in relationship to purpose is the ability to create focus, energy, and passion through communication. They need to develop communication skills that enable them to seek information and ideas in written, audio, and technological formats. They need to develop the ability to find resources and critique them, as well as to conceptualize and synthesize data for varied purposes. And they need to develop communication skills that will enable them to express information and ideas clearly and concisely for audiences in real-world contexts.

Kolis makes the point that the fact-based school does not meet learners' needs and can, in fact, turn learners off. He suggests that one starting point is to focus on purpose as a way to turn the fact-based school on its head. I believe that, because clarifying the purpose of the subject areas is so key a goal, it starts a domino effect of other changes that will and need to follow. Teachers who understand purpose will find themselves rethinking the organization of schools, the frames of the curriculum, and the process of assessment.

There is good news about this in the recently revised model teacher standards of the Interstate New Teacher Assessment and Support Consortium (INTASC 2010). The INTASC standards revision group was guided by a belief that, while maintaining the focus on what teachers need to know, be able to do, and hold as dispositions, the standards need to be reconceptualized in terms of what learners bring: their backgrounds, interests, needs, strengths, and future goals and opportunities.

In the new standards, they encourage teachers to consider the backgrounds K-12 learners bring, from language spoken at home to facility with technology to awareness of global issues. They ask teachers to consider their learners' interests, strengths, and needs. And they invite teachers to consider what learners will need to be prepared for a global marketplace for jobs that have not yet been invented. In other words, one strong goal of the standards is for teachers to make clearer connections between the purpose of the subject areas and learners preparing for twenty-first-century futures.

Major changes in the standards support the kinds of shifts that a focus on purpose requires: a deeper awareness of language and cultural diversity, the power of technology as a learning tool, and rich opportunities in formative assessment. All of which help learners connect their projects and communication to real situations and audiences. Recognizing that understanding of one's discipline is still key, the group sought to foreground the ability to link that discipline with other fields and key skills necessary to expand learning: critical thinking, collaboration, and communication, to name a few.

Finally, while acknowledging the ongoing need for teachers to be able to plan and deliver instruction, the revision calls for a broader practice of collaboration with learners in the design of learning experiences and the development of the learning environment, a way to build a deep sense of purpose indeed.

While I've made the case for twenty-first-century learning as one reason to focus on purpose, I also want to recognize what Frank Smith (1998) wrote about in *The Book of Learning and Forgetting*. In this wonderful little book, Smith also challenges the fact-based school, arguing its approaches systematically obstruct the natural curiosity and inclination to learn that children bring to their first school experience. He talks about the official theory of learning, that learning needs to be painful and difficult and we have to be forced or bribed to do it. He contrasts it to the classic view that learning is natural and enjoyable, and we naturally collaborate when we engage in it.

While Smith does not talk explicitly of purpose, I see echoes of Kolis's thesis in his suggestions that teachers model what they expect of their learners. That means that teachers should engage in the work of the subject area: reading and sharing their interpretations with the class, engaging in experiments in science labs, writing and sharing their writing, creating works of art, and asking questions to which they don't already have an answer.

Those who read this book will likely feel challenged by the picture of the fact-based school and their own acceptance of that picture (and Smith's official theory of learning) as the way things are. But Kolis offers a way out through that first push on the stack of dominoes, the answer to the question, "Why do we (and our learners) have to know this stuff?"

Mary E. Diez
Dean, School of Education
Alverno College
Milwaukee

## REFERENCES

Interstate New Teacher Assessment and Support Consortium. *Model Core Teaching Standards: A Resource for State Dialogue*. Washington DC, 2010.

The Partnership for Twenty-First-Century Learning Skills. "The Book of Learning and Forgetting." Accessed June 3, 2010. http://p21.org/index.php?option=com_content&tasks=view8id=57&Itemid=120.

Resnick, LB. "Nested Learning Systems for the Thinking Curriculum." *Educational Researcher* 39 (2010), 183–197.

Wagner, T. *The Global Achievement Gap: Why Even Our Best Schools Don't Teach the New Survival Skills Our Children Need and What We Can Do About It*. New York: Basic Books, 2008.

# Preface

During my second and third year of teaching, a fear began to grow inside of me. It wasn't a huge fear and, looking back, it was probably not even realistic, but I still remember it vividly. My fear was that my principal would come into my class and ask me, "Why are you teaching this particular topic?"

It was a fear because the answers I knew I could provide were incredibly shallow, and I knew it. I would have been forced to respond in one of the following ways:

1. I just finished chapter 14, and this is chapter 15.
2. All the teachers I am teaching with are teaching this chapter.
3. I like this chapter.

While all qualify as answers, I realized even then that they were terribly weak and demonstrated a very real lack of understanding.

The realization came with experience that my principal would never ask because he himself hadn't a clue. What happened instead was worse. My students began asking a similar question, and it sounded like this, "Mr. Kolis, why do we have to learn this stuff?"

I would like to take this opportunity to apologize to my students from the first eight years of my career: Please forgive me for I knew not what I was doing! Thanks. I needed to do that.

The worst part of it was that I even set myself up. I would say things like, "Science is awesome because it's always changing." It would come back to haunt me when they would ask, "If science is always changing, then why do we have to memorize all this stuff?" I would sputter, hem and haw, and talk about foundational information, but, in reality, my answers continued to be weak and shallow.

I also came to realize that my own reaction to the question changed over the years. At first, I interpreted the question as fear (I didn't know), then as a power issue (I am the king, and they have no right to question my authority), and then ultimately as a lack of understanding issue (I myself did not really know). I came to realize that I myself had asked that question not infrequently when I was a student. I also continue to ask that question at many in-service activities! It was certainly not a content question because I have a double science major and a master's degree in biology, but I still couldn't answer it in a meaningful way (one the students would buy).

I began to ask teachers on a regular basis, "Why do students have to know this specific content?" Good teachers, bad teachers, early elementary teachers, elementary teachers, middle school teachers, and high school teachers, I asked them all. And all gave me the stock answers I had heard as a student.

This caused me to reflect more deeply about my own school experience. You know on the report cards where it has space for teacher comments? Well, I do remember getting the "not working to potential" comment rather frequently throughout most of my schooling, including college where I learned a ton but none of it was reflected in a grade. Why didn't I work up to my potential? Ultimately, I realized my lack of working to potential was related to the question my students were asking me, "Why learn this stuff?"

Those experiences have set me on this journey. Why do students have to learn the material we are asking them to learn? And I don't mean the shallow answers we continue to give them on a daily basis: for a grade, the next course, in college, or when you are an adult. I am talking about answers that are meaningful to our students right now and today, after class, and after school. These answers will help them understand and work up to their potential. That is the journey I invite you to travel with me through this book. Thanks for reading!

Mickey Kolis

# Acknowledgments

First, I would like to publically thank my wife Jeanne. She knows me well and yet still loves me. How special is that! I would also like to thank our three young men—sons Stefan, Ben, and Kory—for their support and pressure to get this book off my computer.

I would also like to thank all the students and educators I have had the opportunity to work with over the years. At Sterling High School, I learned what it meant to be an effective classroom teacher. I would especially like to thank my students in my general science classes. The challenges they provided me helped me grow beyond my comfort zone.

At Montana State University-Northern, I began to learn how universities function and especially loved my education students who were doing the very best they could. I had the exceptional opportunity to work with them in four different courses over four years. The growth they exhibited was passion-affirming. Here at the University of Wisconsin-Eau Claire, I have learned that students still want to change the world in powerful ways. That passion for human growth and the belief that individuals can make a difference makes me confident in the future of our nation.

Last, I would like to thank people whom I have never met, yet have played foundational roles in my thinking over the years: Peter Senge, Alfie Kohn, Leslie Hart, Jay McTighe, Grant Wiggins, Jeannie Oakes, and John Goodlad. I feel as if I know them well because I have thought so much about what they have said about learning!

# Section 1

# And the Point of Schooling Is?
# A Systems Perspective

Schooling across the United States of America is remarkably similar. There are common structures to our schools and common patterns of behavior among the thousands of teachers and millions of students. You can walk into virtually any public school in the United States and feel right at home. In many cases, things have changed so little that you might, in fact, be in the same classroom as when you were in school: the same desks, the same classroom arrangement (except a whiteboard instead of a chalkboard), and, in some cases, the same teacher!

People in the United States are comfortable with those kinds of classrooms because that is where we went to school, and aren't we successful? In fact, most schools today, from kindergarten through graduate school, have changed very little in terms of student learning and classroom instruction over the last thirty years.

Unfortunately, the world has changed, and schools are under tremendous pressure to change as well. The problem is to determine the nature of the change. To truly understand schooling and how it has managed to remain virtually unaffected by the changes around it, we need to examine the current structures of our schools and classrooms, understand how and why they remain in place, and consider the implications that those structures hold for the teachers, the students, and the parents. A quick summary of Senge's (1990, 27–54) thoughts might be "structures of which we are unaware hold us prisoner."

# Chapter 1

# Fact-Based Instruction

## Why It Seems to Work

Let's listen in to virtually any class in American public schools today, especially grades three and up. Feel free to specify the content to any curriculum area or topic you wish.

> *Teacher:* Good morning, class. Today, we are going to start our study of *the parts of the cell*. First, I would like you to read section 1 in chapter 8. Then make a vocabulary list of the words that are in bold print and do the questions at the end of section 1. Tomorrow, I will lecture on *the parts of the cell*. After which, we will do a lab activity where we will use microscopes to identify the parts of the cells. The day after tomorrow, we will have a quiz over section 1 and then move on to section 2. The test over chapter 8 is scheduled for a week from tomorrow. Let's begin.

In most schools and classrooms, textbook recitation is the model of classroom instruction (much less so in early elementary grade levels). To be more specific about the model currently in use, let us name this tradition-teaching model the fact-based model of instruction. The fact-based model is both straightforward and, generally speaking, the model that pops into most people's mind when the term "schooling" is mentioned. It is the general model of instruction that most teachers modify to fit their own particular style and content area. No matter how it is modified, major pieces of the fact-based model usually involve the following components:

## READING

Reading is the backbone of the fact-based model of instruction. The teacher almost always assigns some sort of reading—usually out of a textbook (in literature class students read the same parts of the same book at the same pace)—and implements strategies that attempt to help the students memorize that information. The acquisition of new words, terms, people, or dates, along with their definitions and explanations, provide the basic foundation for learning. To learn the facts that are embedded within the reading is usually the key element in the fact-based model of instruction.

## VOCABULARY

Frequently included in the reading assignment is the task of defining or learning new terms. These words are most frequently in **bold** print, with the definitions either following the term directly or in the side column of the text. It is crucial for the students to learn these new words because the facts are ultimately directly related to this knowledge.

## QUESTIONS

This part of the fact-based model usually involves answering some questions at the end of the assigned section of reading. Questions assigned are either the ones printed in the reading itself at the end of the section or teacher-generated. Generally speaking, the answers to the questions are found sequentially in the reading itself, and the student thinking required in answering those questions is mostly surface-level. The major point of the questions assigned is to emphasize to the students the material that is most important and needs to be learned.

## TEACHER LECTURE WITH NOTETAKING

The teacher leads the discussion (the lecture) and outlines the major points and facts that were in the assigned reading and questions on the board or overhead or through a prepared PowerPoint presentation. In some cases, the teacher also provides the students with fill-in-the-blank outlines or mind maps to help them organize what he is writing on the board. Many teachers include questioning skills and strategies during this lecture portion, and the focus of the lecture centers around the material that was in the reading assignment. Skilled teacher-lecturers include stories, examples, and analogies to help the students make connections between the material at hand and previous student knowledge and experiences.

## QUIZ

Sometime after the teacher lecture, a quiz is given (sometimes even a pop quiz) to find out if the students have in fact learned the material they were supposed to read, answered questions about what the teacher emphasized during their lecture. These quizzes are fact-based, emphasizing the definitions and terms and usually containing true-false, matching, short-answer, or fill-in-the-blank questions. These quizzes are either teacher-generated or come included in most textbook series supplementary materials. Quizzes also serve to emphasize to the students what material is important enough that it might be included on the chapter test.

## ACTIVITY

Frequently during the first or second reading section, some sort of hands-on activity is included. These tightly structured activities reinforce the material that was in the reading and teacher lecture. These classroom activities usually require that the students follow the rules or steps, which when followed correctly, lead them to the one right answer. Verification of the material in the reading is the essential component with these types of classroom activities.

Sometimes hands-on activities, which reinforce the material in the text, are difficult to design. When difficulties arise finding hands-on activities, other classroom activities are frequently utilized. These other classroom activities frequently consist of tasks such as crossword puzzles, word finds, or word scrambles. These tasks all emphasize the importance of the terms and definitions and, once again, point out to the students the facts that are deemed important and need to be learned.

## HOMEWORK

Students need to spend time and energy learning the material they will be expected to know. Class time is limited, so homework is frequently assigned. Reading assignments, section questions, preparing for quizzes, and other classroom tasks that emphasize specific facts are frequently assigned to be completed at home on the student's own time. Parents are expected to monitor the student's behavior in regards to his homework tasks and make sure the tasks are done on time and correctly.

Every other chapter section follows the same pattern until all the sections in the chapter or text have been covered.

## CHAPTER REVIEW: ALL SECTIONS

When all the sections in the chapter or text have been covered, preparation for the assessment, usually a test, begins. Questions at the end of the chapter are assigned, which review the material from each of the previously assigned sections. Different levels of questions make up the categories of review questions. The first group is usually multiple-choice, matching, or fill-in-the-blank. Then there are perhaps short-answer questions. Then there is the application or thinking questions, frequently assigned as extra credit. To supplement these review questions, *Jeopardy* or *Who Wants to Be a Millionaire* is frequently played prior to the test. Each of these activities prepares the student for what is going to be on the test, and what's on those tests are facts.

## TEST

The purpose of these tests is to find out how well the students learned the material they were assigned to read, answered questions about at the end of every section, took classroom notes over, did some activities about, and then reviewed in preparation of the test. The most common format of classroom tests includes some variation of the following: multiple-choice, matching, true-false, short-answer, and essay (still fact-oriented). No matter which format of testing is utilized, they all emphasize the importance of facts.

Testing requirements also require that the teacher treat every student the same. This is frequently interpreted to mean that every student is given the same test (or a scrambled version) the same day and allowed the same amount of time to complete the test. Teachers must also watch carefully during the test to make sure students do not cheat and get credit for learning facts they really don't know.

## TEST GRADES ARE ASSIGNED

Most teachers expect test scores to fall along a distribution similar to a bell-shaped curve: two As, five Bs, twelve Cs, five Ds, and two Fs. If the test grades do not closely resemble that type of distribution, then the teacher will frequently curve the scores, either by lowering the points required for a certain grade (a 90 is the lowest A instead of a 93) or adding points to everyone's scores so the grades fall along the expected distribution. Some classes are, of course, not as bright as other classes or not as bright as students used to be.

## FINAL GRADES ARE ASSIGNED

At some point close to the completion of the quarter or semester, final student grades for the class are assigned based on some combination of how well they have done their homework, the assigned activities, and their performance on quizzes and tests. Different types of activities are assigned different values by individual teachers. Some teachers count homework as a significant part of the final grade, while others heavily emphasize only the quizzes and tests. A single letter is assigned that represents an entire quarter or semester of student learning.

This fact-based model of instruction is introduced to students usually at the beginning of third grade. Math facts, such as addition and subtraction, are emphasized, along with spelling lists, geography facts, and more. This pattern of schooling usually continues throughout the remainder of a student's schooling experience.

# Chapter 2

# Generally Accepted Patterns and Outcomes of Fact-Based Instruction

The fact-based model of instruction is the generally accepted pattern of schooling because it is what we know. It is our mental model or paradigm for how schooling takes place. It is, for the most part, the way the majority of teachers, school board members, and administrators learned when they were students in school. This model of instruction is so common and so unquestioned because, for the most part, we learned that way and it seemed to work for us.

And it's not just the teachers, school board members, and administrators who are comfortable with the fact-based model of instruction. Parents have also gone through their schooling following the same fact-based model. From their experiences, they also have certain expectations of what and how their children should be learning. After all, they are also a function of their schooling as well. So they look for certain kinds of homework, expect certain kinds of tasks and accomplishments, and take pride when their children get good grades and are successful.

## CURRICULUM

A generally accepted curriculum for each content area and grade level also exists. Generally speaking, small groups of content experts get together on a regular basis to review the curriculum in each school district. They look over what is currently being taught; share experiences of how the students are doing; consider what is being covered on the district, state, and national tests; and finally consider facts that they believe every child should know.

Curriculum committees formalize the district curriculum into formats such as introduce-develop-master, share the new curriculum with the teachers and curriculum directors, and then go to the school board for final approval. Once the new curriculum has been approved, district-wide assessments are then modified to meet the new curriculum standards as well.

Players from outside a school district also play major roles in local school district curriculum. States themselves also have content groups, as do most national content groups or learned societies. While not in-district, the process of reviewing curriculum remains basically the same. A group of content experts gets together to discuss what content is worth knowing. Frequently new groups are formed and may exert enormous power on school curriculum. One of the newest content groups to emerge is the technology group. We now have district, state, and national content standards about what and when to teach technology.

National or high-stakes tests also play a critical role in school district and teacher curriculum choices. Knowing what is on the test that ultimately determines the rating of any single school heavily influences how and what is taught and emphasized in the classroom.

Finally, and frequently most importantly, are the textbook companies. Their job is to sell textbooks, and they spend enormous amounts of time and money making their textbook series as attractive as possible. Unfortunately, the textbook and its resources frequently become the curriculum, despite any other curriculum that is supposed to be taught. This happens when facts become the curriculum because the textbooks are ultimately a collection of the facts for any specific topic, all in one easily usable source.

## ASSESSMENT

Within the fact-based model of instruction, there is a generally accepted way of assessing learning as well. Assessment strategies and points of emphasis play a major role in how and what students are taught. In the fact-based model, basic measures of student achievement deal with content facts, and the expectation exists that student learning will and can be assessed by quizzes and tests.

While there has been a dramatic push toward performance assessments (where students are expected to demonstrate their learning through some sort of performance) in many schools, at the opposite end of the assessment spectrum is the national move toward high-stakes testing (where you can't graduate from high school without passing this specific test). Ultimately, what is assessed determines what is important and therefore what is taught.

National testing has come to be accepted and, in fact, mandated in an attempt to hold schools accountable for student learning. Schools are to be held accountable that all students, no matter where they go to school or what their background is, should know the same set of facts. They should also know those facts at the same time (ages and grade levels) and be able to recall those facts in the same way. When teachers know what facts are on the test, they can do an excellent job of preparing their students to do well on those national, high-stakes exams.

## STUDENTS

We also have generally accepted groups of students. With the acceptance of those groups come their generally accepted ways of behaving. If you go into virtually any school, in terms of learning, you will find, generally speaking, three distinct groups of students.

The top group is made up of students who either like the fact-based model of instruction and/or have the innate ability to do it well. Generally speaking, they like school, are good at the fact-based model, and frequently have parents who are positively involved in their learning. They communicate relatively well with adults, do their homework, can memorize effectively, and like getting good grades. Most of these students plan to continue their education after high school in some way or other.

The second tier of students is made up of a mix of those students who want to be in the top group but do not have the innate ability and those who have the innate ability but do not really want to be in the top group. Those students who desire to be in the top group but lack the innate skills work like crazy to get there. They study very hard because they do not have the memorization skills to do it easily. Memorizing is hard work for these students, but they want to be in the top group, so they work and work and work to get there. Many ultimately make the top group in college, where their work ethic can overtake those who have relied upon natural ability alone.

Also in this second tier are those very smart students who constantly ask, even if not aloud, "Why do I have to know this stuff?" They could certainly learn the material if they choose to, but they choose not to. They see no relevance in memorizing all those facts they are quickly going to forget, so they pick and choose what to learn based on their own criteria. When they choose to learn, these students exhibit flashes of brilliance that cause the teacher to wonder why they do not work at that level more frequently. Parents of these students frequently hear from the teacher, "Your child is not working up to his potential." It is true. They aren't.

The bottom tier of students is made up of a wild mix of abilities and disabilities for learning. Frequently, you can find a relatively substantial portion of a school's gifted population in this tier. They have learned that it doesn't pay to be gifted because finishing a task early, from the teacher's perspective, results in being given another of the same sort of task or just waiting until everyone else catches up. They frequently get bad grades in class because, while they ace the tests without studying, they do not do their homework and therefore get zeros for all those grades. They work their way down through the tiers one by one because, to them, memorizing terms and definitions is not worth their time and effort at all.

Also in this lowest tier are many students for whom memorization is a horribly difficult task. Students with learning disabilities, many of whom have been unidentified, and students whose parents do not or cannot provide the help and support the students need are also found frequently in this group.

Many students in this lowest tier frequently cannot read or at least read very, very poorly. Others have been labeled as ADD or ADHD and have been placed in the lowest tier because their other teachers could not get them to work effectively. Still others, at least in high school, are just waiting until they are old enough so they can drop out of school. Teachers who teach these students almost never have a busy schedule during parent conferences because the parents of these students have bailed out of the learning process, just like their children.

## RULES

There are also generally accepted school and classroom rules. No talking unless the teacher calls on you, keep your hands to yourself, no running in the hallways, keep your desk organized, do what you are told, turn in your homework at a specific time in a specific way, sit quietly, and be on time are just a few of the common school rules that exist for the students to follow.

To give these rules some power, there are punishments associated with the lack of following these rules, including teacher reprimands; the loss of privileges such as recess, fun time, free time, or athletics; and the entire category of punishments as well. The latter includes phone calls or e-mails to the parents, time after school, school on Saturdays, visits to the principal or counselor, or even expulsion from the school itself. "Follow the rules or else" is the generally accepted pattern of behavior.

## TEACHER-STUDENT RELATIONSHIPS

Within the fact-based school, there also exists a generally accepted type of relationship between the students and the teacher. This relationship is based on the fact and trust that the teacher knows the facts that are important to know and the teacher has the students' best interest at heart. Teachers would never knowingly do anything to harm the students or do something that wasn't in their best interest. If the student does what he is told to do, learns what the teacher tells him to learn, and does his homework on time and in the prescribed manner, the student will get good grades and be a success.

In the top tier, there is a commitment to this type of relationship because, for the most part, the students agree that grades are a determinant of success later in life. Within the middle tier, the teacher exudes a sense of "I will help you all I can if you would just." For the lowest tier, the relationship is pretty much control and discipline.

## PURPOSE OF EDUCATION

The acceptance of the fact-based model of instruction with its emphasis on facts alone and its generally accepted outcomes also helps to define what educated means. For people whose paradigm of schooling is fact-based, educated has come to mean "to know a lot of facts." Highly educated means "to know even more facts." Students who choose to buy into the fact-based model therefore learn the facts for a variety of reasons.

Some students learn the required facts because they truly like to learn the facts and they like how schools are structured. They are interested in the terms, dates, people, and explanations. They find schooling to be rewarding and worthwhile because they can do the model successfully. They do what the teacher tells them to do, turn in homework when it is required, study what the teacher tells them to study, excel on the tests and quizzes, and are termed "successful students."

Many students and parents believe in the importance of good grades, even if they do not truly believe in the fact-based model of instruction. Some students get good grades or at least make the attempt in order to either get rewards and/or avoid punishment. Honor rolls, student excellence awards, and sometimes prizes accompany good grades.

For some students, the grades themselves are viewed as the reward, in the respect of "I worked hard for this grade." When a particular grade is not received, the incongruity is frequently interpreted by the student as "The teacher had it out for me" or "The teacher doesn't like me." Some parents view grades as so important that they punish their child for not getting a certain grade by strategies such as grounding or removing favorite activities such as computer or TV or sometimes even participation in athletic activities. Good grades matter.

Some students learn what they are told to learn because they or their parents have a clear view of the future. They are motivated by the thought of attending college, sometimes even a specific college or category of college. Some are motivated by the dream of a specific career or job. These students are willing to do almost anything that will get them where they want to go. Frequently for these students, grades play a major role in that low grades might keep them from their dreams, so grades are hugely important to these students.

Another reason that some students learn what they are told to learn is that they trust their teachers and parents. They have either been raised or have it within them that adults have their best interests at heart. Adults would never willingly do or require anything that they truly believed was not in the child's best interest. So they learn the capitols of the states and the times tables, and they read the stories that the teacher assigns. They do their homework, try to get grades that will please the adults in their lives, and trust it will all make sense someday.

If the purpose of schooling is the accumulation of facts, then it does make sense to use the fact-based model of instruction and cover as much material as possible because, the more facts you learn, the more successful you will be. Therefore, fast learners are, in fact, your best learners. Speed does matter. It matters because, when you can learn more facts, you will get better grades. With better grades, you can get into better colleges and universities. Graduating from better schools means better jobs; better jobs virtually guarantee you success as an adult.

It also therefore follows that coverage is more important than depth. A little bit of everything is better than true understanding on fewer, deeper issues. Connecting pieces is rather unimportant compared to getting through the material and is left for the brightest to struggle with on their own. Textbooks become the course because all the really important facts have already been brought together.

In fact, the new textbook series have everything you would need to teach the material and are frequently touted as teacher-proof. They come with overheads, blank mind maps and organizers, fill-in-the-bubble classroom note helpers, test banks, word finds, crossword puzzles, and even teacher notes and PowerPoint slides. Everything you need to teach the fact-based model of instruction is ready and waiting for you.

Because knowing more facts is better, it is crucial that students follow the directions and rules you make. It makes sense for the sake of efficiency. If you do what I tell you to do when I tell you to do it, then we can cover more material, and more is better. Time spent discussing rules and directions is wasted time that could have been better spent on learning more facts. Sometimes, students need some help seeing it that way, so we choose to reward those who follow the rules. This helps all the students to see what good learners look like.

Good learners get good grades, so we single them out by rewarding them with stars on their papers or perhaps some smiley faces. We often praise those students and frequently do it in front of their classmates, that is, to give the others an opportunity to see which student is doing it right. In the higher grades, good learners are rewarded with a high class rank, high grade point averages, and honors such as honor rolls and student of the day, month, and year. The best learners also get the best, most experienced teachers because, in schools, teaching the highest tier is the teacher's reward.

For the sake of efficiency, it also makes sense to sort the good learners from the bad. When the accumulation of facts becomes the purpose of teaching, very clearly, special needs students need to be in someone else's classroom. If their special need is giftedness, they already know the answers and finish their assignments in one-quarter of the time the teacher had allotted. Worst of all, gifted students blow the curve for the rest of the students. They are always ready to move on long before anyone else in the class has even begun.

If their special need is some sort of learning disability which gets in the way of learning the facts, they slow down the class and get in the way. The rest of the class is ready to move on, but they are always way behind. Therefore, they never add anything to the conversation in the classroom. At both ends of the spectrum, those students are better off being in their own classroom with special help.

For the sake of efficiency and to help the students learn as many facts as possible in the time allotted, the parental role becomes one of surrogate teacher. They are the teacher's extension when the child is at home. They are to make sure the reading assignments are finished, questions are answered, homework is completed, and quizzes and tests are prepared for. Failure by the student is interpreted as the failure of the parent.

Doing what the teacher asks ultimately boils down to a trust issue. Students need to trust the teachers. Because they are adults and have been through school, teachers know best. Teachers have been in their place and become an adult. Teachers know how to play the game. Teachers know what it takes to get into college and find a job. Students are too young and immature to make meaningful decisions on their own, so teachers and parents need to make those decisions for them. They aren't doing it to be mean. They do have the student's best interests in mind.

Teachers care deeply and passionately about each of their students and work for very low wages and little or no respect because of their commitment to education. Therefore, when a student asks why he has to know this, it is frequently viewed as a personal affront. They become defensive and interpret the question as a lack of trust. When the teacher does answer the question, his answers naturally support what he knows and believes, the fact-based model of instruction. Knowing more facts is your ticket to future success, so all school and classroom structures are designed to make this happen.

## Chapter 3

# A Skeptic's View of Fact-Based Instruction

While many of the schools across the United States are remarkably similar, that does not necessarily mean they are the best they could be. One of the things it could mean is that there is an acceptance of the status quo. The fact-based model of instruction has its known strengths and weaknesses. Because it is also the model by which most of us learned, we choose to live with it.

The fact-based model of instruction matches our own mental models, and we blissfully ignore the data and facts that do not support the idea that it is in our students' best interests to sustain schooling as it currently exists. We can live with the common problems that are a function of the model because we know what they are and frequently who they will involve and when problems will occur.

A dilemma occurs when both old and new information and data is taken seriously. New perspectives, new models, and new information all can cause us to review the current structures of schools and perhaps cause us to wonder if there might not, in fact, be other ways of structuring our schools.

Perhaps we have learned enough from our experiences to consider new ideas that directly address the weaknesses that might exist in our accepted patterns of behavior within schools. Perhaps we might directly address other patterns that have been overlooked, ignored, or not given credence. Perhaps the acceptable losses, our students who have not bought into the fact-based model and drop out or do not meet their potential, will no longer be viewed as acceptable. Perhaps there is more to schooling than the accumulation of facts.

As we once more listen in to any class in American public schools today, let us also take a look around the room at the students who are present (at least physically).

*Teacher:* Good morning, class. Today, we are going to start our study of the parts of the cell. First, I would like you to read section 1 in chapter 8. Then make a vocabulary list of the words that are in bold print and do the questions at the end of section 1. Tomorrow, I will lecture on the parts of the cell. After which, we will do a lab activity where we will use microscopes to identify the parts of the cells. The day after tomorrow, we will have a quiz over section 1 and then move on to section 2. The test over chapter 8 is scheduled for a week from tomorrow. Let's begin.

Johnny, sitting in the back of the room, is gazing out the window (if his school has windows) and daydreaming about the new skateboarding trick he wants to learn tonight after school. Tameca is writing a note to her best friend, talking about the boy they saw last night at the mall. He was hot-hot-hot, and she's wondering what to do so they can see him again. Shawna has total attention on the teacher, has pre-read the assignment because she knew after the last test that they would begin chapter 8, and wants to be just like her teacher when she grows up. Lance hates school and can't wait to escape and get a job and begin his real life. He sees absolutely no relationship between what the teacher is talking about and making the money that is so important to him. He already has a job after school and works thirty hours a week. In the back, Fred and Jolene are having an animated conversation about the show they watched last night and have not heard anything the teacher has said in the last five minutes. Tom, the class clown, is loving the teacher's presentation. He's adding his own comments and making the kids around him laugh like crazy. He makes fun of his teacher behind her back because she lets him get away with murder because she thinks he's funny. Mark, who reads at the third-grade level, hates this class and school in general. He can build almost anything and has an artist's touch when it comes to building things, but has not gotten a grade higher than a C since fourth grade. He thinks of himself as a school failure. Jesse is doodling and drawing even though she looks to the teacher as if she is taking copious notes. She loves to draw and wonders about a career in art. Frank is a good student, but behind in his homework in other classes, so he is doing his math for next class. He is almost halfway done. If the teacher keeps talking, he will be able to finish and not lose points for a late homework assignment next period.

These students have grown up with fact-based teaching. While they are comfortable with and know what the pattern for learning is, they struggle with its relevance and sometimes with the individual pieces. Success is sometimes elusive for those who have different priorities or skills.

## READING

The backbone of the fact-based model of instruction is reading. If, however, you cannot read, your chances for success in any fact-based school are poor at best. Formal reading instruction has recently fallen prey to the type of thinking that says, "If it's what we expect later, then let's start them earlier."

This earlier-must-be-better type of thinking has previously been characterized by the junior high school model, where, because they teach a particular way in high school, let's get them used to it in junior high school. This model has continued the path. Now many fifth-grade classrooms have content teachers, and the students move from one teacher to the next. This trend will no doubt continue until lectures and content specialists will exist, starting in the third grade.

In many elementary schools, formal reading instruction is now taking place at the kindergarten level. This is problematic from a developmental point of view. The ability to read requires the learner to make sense from abstract symbols. The combinations of abstract symbols (words) represent something that may or may not exist in the concrete. The symbols themselves are difficult to learn, but, without the concrete, making sense of words becomes an exercise in memorization.

Young kids need the concrete first in order to make the connection that these symbols represent the thing they have just held, smelled, felt, or tasted. To see the word "frog" or even read a story about a frog without ever seeing or holding one lacks the concrete connection that allows the learner to make sense of the word as a representation of the real thing. Students who mature later developmentally in this ability are left behind.

When you look at reading groups, which are almost always formed by the end of the first quarter in first grade (Oakes 2005), boys dominate the lowest reading level groups. This may be a function of intelligence, or it might be a function of developmental maturity. Boys develop later than girls on a variety of tasks. When the task is to translate the abstract into sense, boys lag behind.

Unfortunately, once a child is placed in the lowest reading group, he rarely moves up. This happens because the instruction provided by the teacher is significantly different between the high and low group. In the high group, the teacher asks questions focused on prediction (What do you think they will do next?), idea (What do you think they were thinking about?), or evaluation (Did they make the right decision?). In the lowest group, the teacher focuses on the words themselves or perception (What color was the shirt he was wearing?). Once in the lowest group, students can't move up because, with ability grouping, the lesson is, "You can't learn what you haven't been taught."

And it isn't just the questions that matter. When a child is not developmentally able, that means he literally cannot do the task.

Some parents have a thing about their child being potty-trained by a certain age, usually the earlier the better. Being potty-trained early means both the parent and the child are smarter and ahead of the game. The parents study. They ask, and they work with their child. They develop strategies to potty-train their child. When one strategy doesn't work, they find another one and another one and another one.

Finally, they find the one right strategy. Like magic, the child is potty-trained in one day. They tell their friends who try the same strategy, but, unfortunately, it doesn't work for them. Is it really the strategy, or might it be the strategy they were using when their child finally was ready and able to be potty-trained?

In the case of reading, success in school is really linked to the ability to read, and earlier really does mean better. So for the child and the parents, the pressure grows. His teacher tells him it is important, and his parents tell him it is important. He sees his classmates doing the task, and he cannot do it. He wants to, but he can't. Frustrations grow, self-esteem suffers, and expectations change. Then, when he is finally developmentally able to do the task, he no longer wants to. The damage has been done, and the child will almost never catch up to his earlier developing peers.

## VOCABULARY

Knowing the language and the words to use is crucial to success in a fact-based school. The hope is that students who have memorized the words and their definitions will make the jump to understanding. What usually happens is another type of jump from short-term memory to outer space.

Without the concrete experiences, vocabulary lists are just that. They have only one meaning, and that is the definition alone. They do not represent anything real for the learners because it is only a combination of letters. The only way to learn vocabulary words, if you are not a good memorizer, is with extra time and effort. Flash cards, mnemonic strategies, repetition, writing them in sand or shaving cream, and going over them over and over again become the norm for vocabulary tasks.

## QUESTIONS

Generally speaking and rather unfortunately, by the end of second grade, most students have figured out where to find the answers to the questions at the end of a section without truly reading the assignment. Everyone knows the answers are found sequentially in the reading assignment, and frequently in **bold** print as well. The real point must be to make the students write out the answers because thinking on the part of the students is not required.

The questions are almost always surface- or definition-level at best. There is no connection to the student's knowledge bases, previous learning, or any interpretation. Therefore, there really is no real need to read the entire section and understand it as long as you write the answers to the questions, which will most probably be on the test.

## TEACHER LECTURE WITH NOTETAKING

In all reality, there is really no need to read the assignment at all because the teacher is going to tell you what is important to know out of the reading anyway. They tell the students what to know through their lecture. They write down on the board or overhead or tell through PowerPoint slides what the students need to write in their notes, frequently even supplying outline forms or mind maps to help those students who cannot copy effectively.

Good lecturers tell stories, add detail, and provide concrete examples of what was in the reading. Many teachers also ask students questions about the reading, assuming the students have in fact read the material, done the questions, and made their vocabulary list. In fact, the students may have done all they were supposed to do, but, unfortunately, they do not remember the details.

When the teacher engages in this type of activity where the questions focus on the material in the reading, it becomes a waiting and praying game for the students. Usually only two to four students in the class can in fact remember the facts in the reading and therefore successfully answer the teacher questions. Therefore, many students wait out the teacher until he calls upon a student who actually knows the answers and pray the teacher doesn't call on them. (Prayer in school can never be outlawed.)

## QUIZ

Quizzes serve a variety of functions. They act as checkpoints for learning to let the teacher know who is keeping up with the material. They also emphasize to the students which facts are important enough to be tested on. Finally, they provide for more repetition for studying for the students.

Because the emphasis is on the accumulation of facts, the teacher needs to emphasize which facts he deems important and then provide students with ample opportunity to learn them. Quizzes help focus the students on the facts that they will be tested on.

## ACTIVITY

Most classroom lab or other types of activities consist of rule following. They might be hands-on, but they are also brains-off. The students are expected to follow a specific set of instructions and come up with the one right answer. These activities come later in the learning process and therefore serve as verification exercises for material that has already been presented. They are not jumping off points for learning. They are the learning.

For example, let's imagine the topic of learning was bicycles. First, the students would have been required to read about bicycles, answer some questions about the parts, make a vocabulary list of those parts, and participate in a teacher lecture where they drew a bike on the board identifying the important parts. A quiz followed, consisting of a picture of a bike where the student would have to identify the parts using a list of words provided. The lab activity would be to study a real bike or perhaps a model and identify the parts, but not to actually ride it. The point would be for the students to see for themselves what the teacher has already told them: a hands-on, brains-off activity.

## HOMEWORK

Homework may be assigned at any time during the process of learning the facts embedded within the reading. Reading, questions, vocabulary, reports, math facts, spelling, and so forth, all can be assigned as work to be done at home. Homework requires students and their parents to spend their time, resources, and effort learning or practicing a skill or fact that someone has told them is important to learn.

Frequently, homework conflicts with what the student thinks is important enough to spend his time doing. Playing with friends, relaxing, reading what he wants to read, skateboarding, soccer, and music, the list is endless. With so many choices, homework becomes a question of prioritization. If the student sees no value in the task or facts, it becomes the parent's responsibility to help him reprioritize and spend the time doing his homework.

Some parents see and understand the value of learning what the teacher has told the child to learn. They see schooling as a path to getting certain types of jobs and having a particular type of lifestyle. These parents send the message to their child, "Do the work now because it will pay later." They support learning the facts, getting good grades, developing a work ethic, and forming goals for the future.

Parents who do not see the long-term benefit of doing homework struggle to help their children reprioritize. They also believe that other things may be more important than the homework's assigned facts and worksheets. They make an effort to help their child, but that effort is not strengthened by a deep resolve for a specific type of career of future, so they are more easily swayed by their child's desires to spend time doing things that are more relevant today.

Some homework tasks in and of themselves make it difficult for any parent to help his child reprioritize. Crossword puzzles, word finds, and word scrambles are examples of these types of assignments. Unless the child or the parent likes doing that specific task, it is clearly understood to be busy work rather than important challenging work and therefore difficult to prioritize over sports, music, friends, and so forth.

## CHAPTER REVIEW

The chapter review is the teacher's last attempt to emphasize to the students what is important enough to memorize because it will probably be on the test tomorrow. So far, the students have had ample opportunity to learn the material in the reading. They have had reading assignments, vocabulary lists, questions in the reading, worksheets and activities, teacher lecture notes, and, now, one last opportunity, the chapter review. Frequently, this activity might look like *Jeopardy* or, in its newest form, *Who Wants to Be a Millionaire*. Other incarnations also exist, but, no matter the form, the activity emphasizes the facts that the student must know if he is to pass the test tomorrow.

For students who have done the assigned work at the surface level or not at all, preparing for the test becomes a huge issue. They must memorize all the facts that are going to be on the test in one evening. This type of study habit, known as "cramming," is a very common form of test preparation.

Cramming may be relatively successful for the student in the short term, but, then again, that is all that the teacher is really asking. Students who are unfortunate enough to have more than one test on a particular day really are under stress because they have to cram into their heads twice as much material if they are to be successful on each individual test.

## TEST

Most classroom tests are teacher-generated, or the teacher now frequently chooses items from a test bank supplied by the textbook manufacturer. In any case, the teacher selects the items and the format for the test. Some teachers focus almost exclusively on their teacher notes, while others focus on the required reading. Some teachers are very straightforward, while others like the occasional trick question to see who really was paying attention.

Many teachers demonstrate a misunderstanding of the terms "fair" and "equal" and apply them incorrectly to testing. They believe that giving every student the same test, or at least the same test questions, in the same time frame on the same day is fair. It is, in fact, equal and horribly unfair. Equal means treating people the same, while fair means treating them as individuals. For example:

Let's say I have three sons, one fourteen, one twelve, and one eight years old. Imagine that, when I go away on a business trip to Dallas, I tell them I will bring them each back a present. So I do. I buy them all exactly the same thing, a team basketball jersey from the Dallas Mavericks, size adult small. This is equal, but enormously unfair. Fair would be to buy each son something he would individually value, not getting something that meets someone else's needs.

Most testing in today's schools is based on equality and is therefore terribly unfair to many students. Students who have done all the previous assigned work conscientiously usually have no problem doing relatively well on the test. In fact, many students view the test as the challenge. They are ready. They are pumped. Bring it on! They have read what the teacher told them to read, wrote down what the teacher wrote down, and memorized what the teacher told them to memorize. Test taking for these students is a competition, a friendly competition between the teacher's test and the student.

The challenge for the student is to correctly memorize what he believes the teacher is going to ask him on the test. Doing well and getting a high grade is a competition won, a victory earned. The fact that, two days later, he remembers virtually nothing is a moot point.

Students who have not prepared so conscientiously are rather in a bind if they desire a good grade. They cram, but they sometimes might also seek other avenues to do well. Cheating for these students is not unheard of. The grade is what is important, certainly not the learning. In fact, for many of these students, the challenge of cheating effectively is more important than the grade itself.

Students who cheat spend enormous amounts of their time, resources, and effort preparing for the game. They also view testing as a challenge between the teacher and the student. More importantly, they see the game not as a friendly competition, but one where the teacher is holding all the cards and using them to make the students do things he does not want to do. It is literally teacher against student, so anything goes to win.

In these types of classrooms and for these types of students, the most creative activities revolve around outwitting the teacher. Entire texts have been written on the top of erasers. Going through the garbage in hopes of finding draft copies is totally acceptable. Answers written on the bottoms of shoes, the inside of hands, or on the back of the ears of the person sitting in front of them is okay. Just looking at someone else's paper is a technique only for the novice. In reality, if these students spent only a portion of that time actually studying what the teacher told them to study, they would get an A for sure!

Some teachers are aware that some students possess a win-at-all-costs mentality, so they spend enormous amounts of their time, effort, and resources playing the game by working to prevent cheating. They scramble the test questions, run different forms, or watch and monitor the students microscopically during the exam. They even switch seating charts the day of the tests. Testing is a game for the teacher as well. Catching a student cheating proves who is winning the game for the teacher. From the student's perspective, getting away with it wins the game for him.

For other students who do not possess the win-at-all-costs mentality but still want to do relatively well on a test, they depend upon a strategy called luck. They aren't willing to spend a huge amount of time studying everything the teacher suggested might be on the test, so they try to outguess the teacher and only spend a small amount of time studying the right material. Sometimes, this strategy works very well, and they get a very high grade, but, most frequently, doing well really is based on luck. These students always hope for a good grade, but are not crushed by doing poorly because, when they do, it was just bad luck.

Other students exist who want to do well, but might not have the capacity to demonstrate their knowledge through a test format. They may have difficulties reading or comprehending, or they might just be poor memorizers. Time constraints affect many students as well. When a large test is given in a short amount of time, the real question for the teacher is not what you do really know, but what you do know in this specific period of time. For these students, doing poorly on a test emphasizes their deficiencies and ultimately and frequently becomes a self-fulfilling prophecy. They do not believe they can be successful, so they aren't.

Still other students choose to fail. They see no point in memorizing isolated bits of information and then having to memorize even more the next chapter. They see the entire pattern as totally irrelevant and choose not to play the game at all. Passing the class with a minimal amount of effort works for this groups of students until later on when they don't even care about passing at all. These students are just waiting to drop out of school or only want to stay in school so they can be with their friends. Teacher threats such as, "If you

don't do this you will fail," fall upon deaf ears. Many teachers do not understand these students and so let them wait it out.

## TEST GRADES ARE ASSIGNED

Most test grades for any single class do not usually fall along the expected
bell-shaped curve distribution, especially if the teacher uses the 93-86-79-73
percentages to determine grades. Therefore, the teacher frequently curves the
scores to achieve a bell-shaped distribution. This is done by either adding
points to everyone's scores or lowering the curve, usually based upon the
highest student score.

By basing the curve upon the highest student's score, everyone's grade in
the class depends upon how well the smartest student does on any particular
test. This means that, if a student scores an 85, that might be an A or B or C
depending on how the other students in the class do on the test.

The student who consistently blows the curve for the other students by
scoring way above everyone else is not looked upon with favor by his classmates. Grades are therefore awarded not based on how much a student knows,
but by how much they know compared to everyone else in the class. This
strategy pits student against student and is done for sorting purposes rather
than for learning.

In reality, after the very first test in a class, the class and individual distribution of grades on tests change very little. A student who gets a B or an A
or a D on the very first test in any teacher's class will generally continue to
get the same grades on all the rest of the tests in that class for that teacher.
When a change does occur, it is most frequently downward. This pattern
exists because students who do well know how to play the game while others
either do not want to play or have chosen to play a different game altogether.
Schools could save an enormous amount of time and effort by giving only the
first test and assigning all grades on that basis alone.

## FINAL GRADES ARE ASSIGNED

As they exist today, grades are the ultimate hammer in schools. They communicate very clearly to students, parents, and the community what is and
what is not important. Grades today are based very simply upon memorizing
the facts that the teacher tells you to memorize when they tell you to do it in
a way they have determined. Teachers give students multiple opportunities
to figure out what is important and worthy of being memorized. They assign

homework, quizzes, and tests. They provide activities and review sessions. They even frequently directly tell the students what is going to be on the test, and still students fail or do poorly.

Good grades generally tell us who the good memorizers are, who has connected with the teacher, who has bought into the system, and who knows how to play the game. Grades are used to sort our students, but do not indicate who the best thinkers are because memorizing is not thinking.

Memorizing is a skill unto itself and of very little use in the world outside of schools. Memorizing is not thinking, doing, planning, or implementing. It's not creative, and it's not a measure of intelligence. Being a star on *Jeopardy* does not make you brilliant. It means you know a lot of trivia.

And is it even truly possible to represent all the learning that has occurred over the course of eighteen weeks through the use of a single letter? Can one letter possibly represent all the learning that has hopefully taken place? What about things learned like perseverance, creativity, getting along with others, overcoming learning deficiencies and barriers, and effort, just to name a few? These lifelong learning characteristics are clearly not valued in schools because there is absolutely no way they affect a student's grade. They might be included on the report card as a teacher comment, but do not matter in class rank or GPA calculations.

Grades do provide us with an excellent and easy way to sort students, like eggs or beef. It is a value system because it allows us to make judgments about the student quickly and easily. An A student is this kind of person who has this kind of future while an F student is a very different kind of person with a very different kind of future.

Grades become a sort of self-fulfilling prophecy because those at the top also get the most and best resources. The top group gets the best, most experienced teachers. They get to answer significantly different kinds of questions. They have the strongest parental support. They get the most field trips and get to participate in the most extracurricular activities. Remember, if you get bad grades, the punishment is no extracurricular activities.

Grades determine class rank and GPA and, therefore, scholarship opportunities and awards. Besides those factors, colleges like grades. Grades make it easy to see who the good students are, those with high GPA and, therefore, high class rank.

Sometimes, because tough high school classes like calculus and Advanced Placement courses make it hard to get good grades like As, some high schools utilize a special way of calculating GPA. Those tough courses have a different scale for determining GPA. This special formula means that, on a four-point scale, in these tough classes, an A is worth five points, a B is worth four points, and a C is worth three points. This is called "weighting grades."

Therefore, not only does the student learn more facts that virtually guarantee success in getting into a college, they also get to reduce the risk of hurting their GPA while they do it. It doesn't stop there. Many scholarships also have overall GPA and class rank as their main criteria.

When grades are the sole measure of achievement in schools and those grades are a function of the fact-based model of instruction, schools become institutions geared to sorting students rather than institutions geared for learning.

# Chapter 4

# Generally Ignored Patterns and Outcomes of Fact-Based Instruction

The fact-based model of instruction is the prevalent model used in the schools. Within that focus, it can be said it does its job very well. There are associated patterns of behavior that exist when the model is used, both obvious and hidden. For any accepted pattern of behavior, alternatives exist, but, once a model is generally accepted and the longer it remains unquestioned, the more hidden and accepted are the detriments.

In the case of schooling, those who do not benefit or those who struggle with the accepted form of instruction take the hit. They pay the price with lowered expectations and accept poor quality. They are encouraged to drop out so their questions do not have to be addressed. This results in wasted potential of our youth and the overall quality of our country's future.

When questioning what other generally ignored patterns exist, the key question is, "Are facts really the point of schooling?" If the answered is not an unequivocal yes, then the search may continue for hidden patterns and outcomes.

## CURRICULUM

Having a generally accepted curriculum between classrooms and schools is not a detriment to our students. What might be considered a detriment is the process by which curriculum is made and the effects upon teachers and therefore our students. When the small group of content experts gets together to decide upon the new and improved curriculum, each content group meets independently. They each follow the same pattern of behavior, and the small group is usually comprised of content experts who are passionate about their content area.

An unexpected outcome of the curricular process is that the curriculum list of facts, especially for the elementary teacher, grows larger every review. Each and every curriculum group tells the teacher to teach all the facts he is currently teaching, plus some new ones. And while the list of facts grows, the amount of time and resources available to the teachers remains the same. This generalized pattern of behavior happens across virtually every school across the nation, including the university systems.

And this pattern exists outside the curriculum groups as well. Other interested parties and groups within a district also influence the curriculum in the same way, asking for their interest areas to be included. There are now learning styles groups, Native American groups, multiple intelligences groups, character-building groups, gifted and talented groups, music, dance, drama, and vocational education groups, each behaving in exactly the same way.

Because we are living in the information age and the amount of information is increasing rapidly, we can expect new groups to continue to form. We would expect them to follow the same process as the other groups already in place and for the school curriculum to continue to grow and grow and grow.

A relatively new player into school curriculum, and one that may ultimately overpower all the other players, is the national high-stakes exam. When the quality of learning is measured by a student's performance on one exam, what is on that exam ultimately decides what is taught by each teacher within each school. Period, end of sentence.

This pattern of enormous growth within the school curriculum occurs and will continue to occur because, when facts are the sole purpose of schooling, everyone wants his facts included. In fact, the amount of facts included from each group represents the power each group brings to bear on what is taught.

The more powerful the curriculum group, the more it can push its own agenda and get more of its facts included in the school curriculum. This is a power issue because, while the amount of curriculum has grown, the amount of time to teach it has not. The pattern of behavior for curriculum groups therefore results in a competition between what facts can be covered in the amount of time each teacher has.

The ultimate outcome of the current curricular process is that teachers are required to teach more and more and more facts in the same amount of time, which results in more and more fragmentation of material. We don't go deeper. We just do more. The students are just expected to learn more and more facts that have no meaning to them.

## ASSESSMENT

While testing may be the most common and accepted way to assess learning, fact-based tests cannot and do not measure the ability to do. They emphasize facts that currently exist and place a heavy emphasis on regurgitating those facts exactly as they were taught with no thinking, analyzing, application, and action required. "Memorize what I tell you to memorize because your grade depends upon it" is the hidden pattern and outcome of testing.

Thinking for yourself is unimportant, as is creativity, critical thinking, or curiosity. Cramming works because the facts are only important for a short period of time. Then new facts become important and then even newer facts and so on and so on. All facts are given equal weight in terms of importance, so the student treats them all the same. Memorize and forget is the pattern most students utilize when it comes to testing.

Fact-based tests allow for no utilization of different ways of knowing. Everyone is given the same test on the same day and the same amount of time to complete it. Students who wish to do well are frequently victims of test anxiety because they understand the importance of a certain letter grade. Students who work slower also take a hit because the real message to the students is that we want to know how much you can recall in a specific amount of time, not just what you know. Time frames are incredibly important in testing and, when adjusted, play havoc for the teacher.

One year when I was a public school teacher and still teaching traditional fact-based science, a mother came in and asked if her son could have more time to take his tests. She said he knew the material, but worked slower than most, but he could do well on the tests if given more time.

This started me thinking. I thought, "If I gave him more time, wouldn't everybody want more time? And then, where would the extra time come from?" I would have to make him come in after school because the next period's teacher would get mad if I kept him after my time was over. Not only that, but if I let him come in after school, wouldn't he then cheat and study during the classes in between my class and after school because he had already seen the test questions? Also, wouldn't it cause a plague of students wanting more time as well? It would mess up everything when the tests would be graded. Time after school would have to be reallocated. I would have to explain to all the other students. Then how would I explain giving him more time? Wouldn't that be unfair to the other students?

But then again, what did I want? Did I want to find out what he knew, or did I want to find out what he knew in a specific amount of time? What was fair, and what was equal? I had good friends in college who clearly knew more facts than I did, but choked on tests. What was that all about anyway?

That one mother's request turned out to be a cathartic experience in my life as a teacher. It ultimately changed everything in my classroom.

Earning grades in the fact-based model is really a measure of how well you do what the teacher tells you to do and memorize what the teacher tells you to memorize in the time frame the teacher gives you. The ability to memorize is infrequently an intelligence issue.

Many teachers give the students every opportunity to be successful on the test. Frequently before a test, the teachers give students the topics to be tested and sometimes even the questions themselves. The answers are right in the lecture notes, and they come right off the quizzes. Some even go so far as to allow students to retake certain quizzes and tests to raise their scores.

When it is all said and done, preparing for tests and memorizing the facts you are being asked to memorize is a relevance issue. Many students see no relevance in memorizing the facts, so they do not put in the time, resources, or effort to do it well. But, because grades are so important and they want good grades, cheating becomes a common pattern of behavior.

National norm-referenced tests are a different beast altogether because they only focus on what students do not know. Their job is to sort the students. Any test item that too many students get correct is omitted from the test altogether. Norm-referenced tests are built and designed to separate students into a bell-shaped curve, not to find out what they know. For any well-designed norm-referenced test, half of the students will be above average. Half will be below average. It is a competition of student against student, pure and simple. Or, when used as a measure of school accountability, it is school against school.

## STUDENTS

The fact-based model of instruction helps separate students into relatively distinct groups. Within the top tier of students are those who have learned how to play the game and/or have a goal in mind, which makes public school and its emphasis on facts a stepping stone to future success, a hurdle to be overcome. They know all about the importance of grades, how GPA is calculated, and where they stand in terms of class rank. The top-tier students ultimately care little about learning as long as they get good grades. They understand that there is a competition to get into the best colleges and into certain careers. They, along with their parents, work the system to their best interests.

At the high school where I used to teach, we used to have a grading device known as weighted grades. Certain classes were designated as having these weighted grades, which meant that, when it came time to determine GPA and class rank, an A was given five points on a four-point scale and a B was four points on a four-point scale. These were classes such as calculus, advanced biology, and, of course, all Advanced Placement courses. The idea was that the top students were staying away from these tough courses because they might get a B or, heaven forbid, even a C, so it would lower their GPA and class rank. So to entice them to take a tough course, they were rewarded with more points.

Courses that, of course, were never awarded special status were things like home economics, woodworking, physical education, health, or art. What ultimately happened was that the top students stopped taking any courses that weren't weighted because any non-weighted course lowered their overall GPA! So the top students, who had the best chance to get into the college of their choice anyway, got the biggest break in terms of grading as well.

By the time these students are in their later years in high school, learning has taken a distant backseat to getting a high grade. Top-tier students have the system down pat. For the most part, they can get good grades without too much thinking. These students never ask, "Why do I have to know this stuff?" They recognize the importance of the grade and what it means to their future. In fact, they are so comfortable with the rules of the game that they themselves don't want the rules (school) changed while they are still in attendance.

The second tier of students is made up of a mix of students who want to be in the top group but might lack the ability and those who have the ability but do not want to play the top group game. For those who want to be in the top group, hard work is a way of life. They come in to school early and stay late. They love teachers who give extra credit and are willing to do almost anything if they can just get the opportunity to be in the top group.

For those who have the ability but not the drive to be in the top group, they exhibit and tantalize their teachers and parents with flashes of brilliance. They might get an A on every test, but never do their homework. Their thinking is that, if they get an A on the test, then why do they have to do the day-to-day assignments? They know the material. And isn't that really the point?

The bottom tier of students has the lowest expectations demanded of them. Being in class and not being a discipline problem is frequently the highest hope for these students. Most high school dropouts, as well as many students who receive a GED, come from this group. They frequently start work at jobs early in their high school years, and they make it clear that they do not wish to be in school, except, of course, for the social aspect of schooling.

Bottom-tier students see no relevance to the fact-based model of instruction, so their actions follow their convictions. In fact, by the time these students are in high school, they frequently make fun of their gifted friends who have to spend hours each evening doing homework because, in the low-track classes, homework is never even assigned because it's all done in class.

Students with learning disabilities, students who can't read, and students who have real-life problems can also be found in this lowest tier. Typically by fifth grade, parents of these students have bailed because they have tried everything they could to no avail. They quite literally do not know what to do with their children. The hugest majority of these students are male, usually upwards of 90 percent. In fact, it is not unusual to have a gender distribution of eighteen boys and two girls in a low-track class.

Classroom discipline is a huge issue. Most school dropouts and most major school discipline problems come from this tier. These students constantly ask, "Why do I have to know this stuff?" If your answer doesn't work for them, common responses include, "That's stupid!" or "This sucks!" They frequently lack the social skill of disagreeing politely. For teachers who truly care about these students, they are rewarded with loyalty literally unto death. These students have come to believe they cannot be successful. Those teachers who convince them otherwise, often despite the students themselves, are the school's ultimate heroes.

These tiers exist, and they are usually formed by the end of the first quarter of first grade. The original basis for the tiers is based on reading ability (bluebirds, robins, and crows) and continues because so much of schooling and the learning of facts is based upon the ability to read. Students who are poor readers always end up in the lowest tier, period.

## RULES

Rules are made to get people to behave in certain ways for certain reasons, and the rules in schools are no exception. Sit quietly, hands to yourself, no cheating, no running, no bad language, no sloppy desks or binders, no talking without permission, no skipping school, no tardies, no absences … no, no, no. The rules in schools are made to help students get along and be as successful as possible in learning the facts. Another unwritten rule is no fun as well.

Most school rules are not directly related to learning. They are really about adult convenience issues. Does a quiet classroom really mean that learning is taking place? What about the idea that, by processing verbally and sharing ideas and perspectives, everyone in the group benefits and might actually remember something for more than forty-eight hours? Are most adult workplaces quiet? And are the adults there expected to work independently without communicating with their co-workers?

Schools expect even very young people to act as some sort of ideal mini-adult. This is an ideal because I have yet to see a group of teachers at any in-service behave in the way they expect their own students to behave. Do they sit quietly? Are they on task? Are they even paying attention to the speaker? Very few adults can behave the way we expect even an eight year old to behave.

And to get them to follow these rules, there are, of course, punishments, more commonly known as "consequences." Embarrassment is usually a part of the punishment as well as depriving the student of something they value, for example, their own time after school, time before school, recess time, playtime, weekend time, or any time the student would rather be somewhere else besides school. What can be a worse punishment than having to spend more time somewhere you hate?

That, of course, is the hidden message with most school punishments. School is already a punishment, so, when we punish you, you have to spend more time in school. School punishments sometimes make no sense at all and do not demonstrate a true depth of understanding.

Some teachers I have seen expect their students to sit quietly all day long. When they don't, I have heard the following threat, "If you kids don't stop squirming around and sit quietly, you will lose your recess time." Who is punishing whom?

The problem with the rules in schools is that they exist without understanding. There is no dialogue between teacher and students about why the rules exist and why it is to everyone's, not just the teacher's, benefit to follow the rules or change them if necessary. A wonderful opportunity to learn about rule-making is lost, so a different game ensues. This game follows the same pattern as the curriculum game.

Some students view the school rules and punishments as a study guide. They search and experiment until they find what is not prohibited and then do that particular thing. When caught and told it is against the rules, they confidently reply that the specific behavior is not prohibited. And they are right. So the next time the school rules are reviewed, something more is added to the prohibited list. The list of don'ts always grows with each review.

The other list that grows is the punishment list. School punishments continue to get harsher. Students who are more resistant continue to accept the punishments in order to do what they want to do. Time after school was not enough, so in-school suspensions came into being. When that wasn't bad enough, Saturday suspensions came into being. Out-of-school suspensions may work because students are separated from the social aspect of schooling. And finally, for those students who hate school and don't want to be there, there's expulsion. The only actual punishment that exists for these students is not being with their friends.

If rules and punishments that currently exist in schools really worked, wouldn't the students who misbehave the most be cured by the end of the first semester or certainly no later than the end of the year? In reality, aren't the kids who are naughty in second grade almost always the same ones who were naughty in first grade and so on and so on? Who is not learning? Doing the same thing over and over again and expecting different results is said to be a sign of insanity.

Rule following for rule following's sake with no deep thought, explanation, or purpose provided clearly demonstrates a lack of respect for the individual. Students are treated like little children, which is okay when they are little children. The question finally becomes, "How are they growing into adults?" Schools give students no real responsibilities to provide for this type of growth. And don't even mention student council where the only real choice they get to make is the theme for Homecoming.

Real responsibilities mean real consequences without the adults saving them. To clarify, a consequence is a natural result of the action taken. For example, if you break a window, the natural consequence would be to first clean up the mess and then replace the window. A punishment is an arbitrary action not related to the initial action. If you break a window, you sit in a corner, serve detention, or stay after school. Punishment makes the person sorry … sorry he got caught. Natural consequences teach the relationship between what they did and what the result might be.

Rules need to exist so humans can work effectively with one another. Rules also need to exist for everyone's benefit. In the case of schools, that includes the learning opportunities for our children.

## TEACHER-STUDENT RELATIONSHIPS

The fact-based model of instruction ultimately results in a you-versus-me mentality (teacher versus student) and classroom environment. This happens because the teacher is viewed as holding all the cards in the game. They have all the facts. They assign the homework. They make the tests and quizzes, and they assign the grades. Schooling is teacher-oriented in that, because teachers hold all the cards and make all the rules, they ultimately determine the structure of the classroom. Asking students to make the classroom rules after first grade is a sham because, by then, they have already learned the rules. The way we know this is that the rules the students come up with are never a surprise.

The game continues because the teacher also appears to know all the answers and will only share when he wants to. I have it, and you need it. I'm going to give it to you when I think you are ready for it, whether you like it or not. Facts are doled out piecemeal and generally without context. Facts are important for fact's sake. If they have something to do with the students' lives outside of school, it is pure luck.

This type of thinking is seen very clearly with the game mentality of testing. What's really important to know about the teacher is the teacher's model of testing. Do the questions come from the lecture notes, the reading, and the questions in the text? And how frequently does the teacher ask trick questions that were in the reading and notes, but were so trivial that only one person per class got it right?

The you-versus-me classroom environment is easily observed by noticing the classroom rules that the teacher has established. Students are expected to sit for more than six hours per day in a desk that would make an adult cry like a baby. Not only that, students are expected to sit still. They are not to fidget or squirm because, if they do, they might lose their recess, where they might actually burn off some of those fidgets. Students are also not allowed to speak to their neighbors, even when sitting within two feet of other people.

Students are expected to do what they are told and not allowed to ask any meaningful questions. They are given little or no background. They are certainly not told the reasons why this material is important to learn in a way that makes sense to the learner. Students are expected to wait for relevance until they are an adult, as if having a job, spouse, or child answers the relevance issues. Unfortunately, no button turns on that magically transforms you into an adult.

What would happen if you didn't believe that facts were the most important part of education? What if you believed that there might be something more important, something deeper at stake in education?

To question the idea that the quantity of facts is a determinant of the term "educated" also means that the definition of educated itself might be something else. For example, looking up the word "educate" in the dictionary leads one to this definition, "to lead, to develop the knowledge, skill or character of (by formal schooling)." Perhaps the idea that isolated facts that probably can't be recalled anyway equals knowledge needs to be revisited. The question might be, "What are they becoming knowledgeable about?"

To question the belief that facts are the end in mind also then leads to the question of, "Which facts are then truly important to know?" Is every fact truly of equal weight, or are some facts truly essential to know? Do teachers have the right to make someone memorize the facts they like just because they like them? In other words, if I happened to really like cell structure and function, Shakespeare, geometry, or dodgeball, does that really give me the right and power to give someone a grade based on him memorizing what I think is important? And if all facts are of equal value, then what is wrong with the facts that students like?

To question fact-based learning also then questions the ability of a single letter to represent all learning for a quarter or a semester. Is that even truly possible? Can one single letter really represent any person's potential, ability, growth, or learning?

Schools frequently say they want students to be responsible, but they are too young so it becomes a wait issue. Wait until I'm ready to give you the responsibility rather than give you the responsibility when you are ready to learn (you ask). It looks like this:

I like to garden, so I spend time gardening in the spring and summer. My kids see me out there. They frequently see my wife join me. Sometimes, especially when they are very young, they want to participate. Either I let them help me garden when they want to, or I end up doing it all myself because, when I am ready to let them garden, chances are, they won't want to.

And yes, it takes three times as long. Yes, I sometimes have to replant after they think the beans are weeds. Yes, they learn to garden on their own. To learn responsibility means you have to have opportunities to live with the consequences. Remember the magic button? People need the opportunity to grow into responsibility.

This lack of trust on the part of adults toward the students ultimately results in the students exhibiting a lack of trust in adults. Teachers have what you need, but won't give it to you. Adults think school is a game for the students to figure out. They don't care about your needs. Their needs outweigh yours. Just do what they tell you, and be sure to leave your cares at the door. It's immaterial that your dad was thrown in jail last night for hitting your mom. Only things that interest them are important. Their stories are okay, but yours are irrelevant. Besides that, "What's a record player anyway?"

Students are also expected to ignore their own questions and leave their problems at the door. They are to stay on task for the entire day and to quit trying to get the teacher off task by asking interesting, but irrelevant questions. Finally, students have to ask if they may go to the bathroom, and they are sometimes told no. If that is not power, then what is?

Fact-based teaching also basically ignores the individual and attempts to force people to ignore their own needs. Following directions is an okay strategy for safety issues. It's not an exceptionally good strategy on the higher end of thinking tasks. Having everyone learn the same facts the same way in the same time frame also takes away those things that make us unique and special. Our interests and our experiences play no role in this type of teaching.

Multiple intelligences (Gardner 1983), learning styles, and all the combinations therein become add-on issues to the learning tasks for the teachers. You do what you have always done, but you must also add these specific words and these specific types of activities into the model you are already using.

And it's not just the teachers who suffer from the emphasis on facts. Parents come to be viewed as adults because their role changes as well. In early elementary grades, the parent's role is one of support, helping the child to read stories, color inside the lines, begin to write, play well with others, and grow and develop.

Beginning in third grade with the shifting emphasis to memorizing isolated facts, the role of parent as child advocate changes from support of the child to an extension of teacher. It becomes a parental study skills issue, where it is now the parent's job to help the teacher make sure the student knows math facts, spelling lists, geography, ad nauseam.

Parents are expected to become the teacher's helper in the fact-based model of instruction rather than the student's supporter. This happens even when parents might not have an in-depth content knowledge. Remember, they learned through the fact-based model as well, so most of those facts are long forgotten.

Students frequently begin to view parent's love as conditional, from "I love you for you" to "I love you if you do this." I love you when you get that kind of grade and make the honor roll so I can put on the bumper sticker that says, "My student is on the honor roll at ..." Success in school becomes the measuring stick for love. Parents are put into a no-win situation because they cannot change teacher behavior and the fact-based model of instruction.

Perhaps the largest issue when students are subjected to the fact-based model of instruction is the virtually total lack of relevance. Topics of study are not related to student life concerns, needs, or developmental issues. There is no connection between the topic of study and what the individuals are concerned with at that point in time.

Student problems, questions relating to sexuality (their own, others, and the interplay between the two), questions related to maturity (rites of passage, changing expectations, and the interplay between freedom and responsibility), questions dealing with power and adultness are never addressed directly. So students ask, "Why do I have to know this stuff?" They are given reasons that do not meet their needs.

The emphasis on learning the facts results in a system where power struggles are part of the everyday experience. The teacher's role is making sure everyone toes the line and follows the rules: no talking, no writing notes, no squirming, no looking out the windows (if the school even has them), no running in the hallways, stay on task, and get your homework done. If you don't, you will be a failure in life. All this is from an adult they are expected to love and respect.

Therefore, most discipline problems result when students are trying to tell the teacher in not-so subtle ways, "This material does not interest me!" or "Learning all these isolated facts does not meet my needs." The question is not, "Why are they so bad and naughty?" but "What needs do my students have that are not being met?"

The fact-based model of instruction and the fact-based system that supports it is deeply entrenched in the schools and within the minds of those who have been educated through that model. It worked for us, or at least we survived to go on and become productive adults. Unfortunately, times are changing.

We are living in the information age. The sheer quantity of information (facts) in the world is doubling at an ever-increasing rate. Our capacity to learn all the facts is quickly becoming overwhelmed.

Many people have come to hate school because they see no relevance. School comes to be seen as a restrictive place where students have no power and no ownership of their own learning. They feel isolated within their peer groups, and many lack the feeling of success in regards to their ability to learn. Their needs are not being met because there is no connection between what they are being asked to learn to their personal lives outside of school.

To look at where we have been with its strengths and weaknesses and to deeply consider new information that might be applied to teaching and learning might lead us to believe that alternatives to the fact-based system exist. These alternatives must go beyond the idea of more to the idea of deeper if we are to truly educate our young for a changing world. Factors such as perseverance and work ethic, relationships, creativity, critical thinking, following dreams, and self-fulfillment must be a part of the education system for that world.

*Section 2*

# Purposes Defined

# Chapter 5

# Why Purpose Is Important

We are a function or result of our own schooling experience. Our experiences and how we dealt with them become our view, our paradigm (mental model) of what schools are and should be. Therefore, generally speaking, we don't know what the point is if it isn't the accumulation of facts. There is also no general agreement in our country on what the outcome of schooling really is or even what it needs to be. This lack of focus buffets schools and teachers with changing demands. You name it—socialization, technology, health services, drug education, content issues, and inclusion—schools have become responsible for teaching it. A point in every direction is the same as no point at all.

Without a powerful purpose, there is nothing. We first head in this direction, then another direction, and then yet another direction, and the students pay the price. We fragment into small groups, push our own agendas, and wonder why the other groups do not see it our way. Parents become people we have to deal with rather than partners working to help every child be as successful as he can be. School administrators and teachers are enemies, along with school board members and legislators.

We must find deep, meaningful answers to, "Why do we have to know this stuff?" Until we do, there will be no common purpose. It is a moral issue for adults and teachers because, until we do, we cannot hope to meet the needs of our children. Because we are functions of our own school experiences, we must look elsewhere for examples of what learning might be about.

We could look at life outside the schools and ask:

- What does life require from us in terms of learning?
- What is required in life to be successful, happy, productive members of society?
- What skills and characteristics does it take to live in a rapidly changing world?

We could even look at extracurricular activities such as sports, clubs, school newspapers, and yearbooks and ask, "Why do kids spend so much of their time, effort, and resources participating in these activities?" And we might also want to study the "non-core" content areas such as vocational education, band, choir, and art to see what learnings we might glean from these types of learning experiences.

In short, do we want our children to leave school being good rule followers and good memorizers (and forgetters) and do whatever others in positions of power tell them to do? Do we really want our children to never question authority or do anything for a grade or money? Do we really want our children to always follow someone else's vision because they cannot craft their own? If the answers to those questions are problematic, then perhaps there might be something of deeper value that our schools could help our children learn.

Generally speaking, all schools teach the following content areas (all are fragmented within themselves): language arts, social studies, mathematics, and science. Most schools also teach some combination of the following content areas as well: music, art, foreign language, health/physical education, and vocational education.

Because every school across the country teaches the same sort of curriculum, there must be something deep and powerful within that particular content. The question is, "What is the deep purpose to each content area?" We need to know the answers so we may convince our children that what we are asking them to learn is truly worthy of their time, effort, and resources. Each content area purpose must be at the core of the spiraling curriculum, relevant to students of every age and be able to answer the question, "Why do I have to know this?"

We are searching for big, deep patterns within each content area, which allow us to meet individual learner needs today. They must be the core of the spiraling curriculum, providing purpose and a context for the differing skills that spiral around the core. These reasons must be intrinsically motivating when tailored to learner needs and infinitely modify-able.

For our model and definition of learning, let us consider the type of learning that happens naturally, outside the school setting. Generally speaking, we can say that humans are learning machines (Diamond and Hopson 1998; Hart 1983; Darling-Hammond et al. 2008; Jensen 1998; Sylwester 1995; Kotulak 1997; Sousa 2001). Learning begins at birth for both the parent and the child and, for the most part, continues for a large portion of a person's life. Let us use the following scenario for an example:

Suppose you are six years old and growing up outside an isolated town in Montana, fifty miles from the nearest town. Your family raises black Labrador Retrievers. You rarely go to town, but do regularly play, feed, and help take care of your family's six to twenty dogs. You pet them, name them, play with them, and brush them. They are what you know.

One day, you go with your family to a large town and see a Chihuahua. You ask what that animal is, because, for absolutely sure, the first word out of your mouth is not "dog." Dogs are black, weigh about 75 pounds, have long tails, and are about three feet tall. This thing weighs about four pounds and looks like a rat. To you, the word "dog" represents (the picture it brings forth in your mind) a totally different animal.

The same would be true if confronted with a Great Dane and perhaps even a Dachshund. What you know is defined by your experiences.

Let us therefore represent an experience as the following:

Each experience is both colored by the person's genetic makeup as well as his previous experiences.

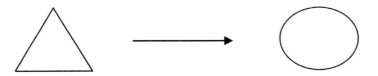

Each circle represents a concept and is usually associated with a label (a name). Each word therefore represents a concept. *Black Lab* would be a relatively narrow concept whereas *dog* would be a much larger concept. When a concept or generalization is based only on one experience (or one type of similar experiences), the concept is understood at a relatively shallow level.

The three connected triangles represent multiple experiences (not just three) with the same concept or object. The more similar the multiple experiences, the shallower the understanding of the concept. In our story, the young person had multiple experiences with dogs, but the experiences were very similar, resulting in an understanding of *dog* as the same as *black Lab*. To truly understand, in depth, it would be best to understand the concept of *dog* by experiencing multiple different dogs multiple times. Generally speaking, it can be said that, the more diverse the experiences, the better for a deep understanding of the concept of *dog* to emerge.

## Chapter 6

# The Purpose of Language Arts

The study of language arts is not about spelling, especially not lists from a book that have no context. It is not about vocabulary lists, sentences, sentence diagramming, grammar, or memorizing the teacher's interpretation of a written work. Each of these activities is not poor teaching in and of itself. The lack of context (purpose) causes the activity to lose relevance.

The content area purpose for teaching all language arts is the expression of the human experience through words. It's in the words, the art of using language.

Effective communication is a clarity issue. Because we are humans, it is ultimately a two-way interaction: writer-reader and/or speaker-listener. Communication is relationship-oriented and connection-based.

When we speak and write, we attempt to be as clear as possible, but the listener and reader get in the way. Their experiences, their definitions of words and concepts, and their perceptions are different from ours, so miscommunication is the result. This becomes an intrinsic motivational issue because, at the deepest level, humans do not like to be misunderstood. The art of using language then is to clearly communicate ideas, thoughts, and concepts from one person to another.

Speaking and writing utilize symbols (letters, words, and sounds), and those symbols represent something, frequently something concrete or real, especially in early grades. The basic assumption made in schools by teachers is that students have had the same experiences they have had, so they have a concrete base from which to build their representations.

When teachers go from one experience with a concept directly to letters (which represent the concept), very frequently, the pictures in the teacher's head and the students' heads are not anywhere near the same. They are different sizes, colors, and textures and have different uses and values. Their stories are not your stories.

If the teacher truly wants the students to understand the concept of "dog-ness," they must provide students with experiences with little dogs, big dogs, brown dogs, white dogs, long-haired dogs, short-haired dogs, working dogs, show dogs, and just plain family dogs. The word "dog" represents them all, not just black Labs.

Using pictures helps the concept become more general and deeper, but not nearly as much as having the multiple diverse experiences. Pictures themselves are two-dimensional representations of something, so showing a group of students a picture of a Great Dane and saying "dog," while better than just writing the words on the board, is nothing like actually experiencing a Great Dane. And finally, when there is no concrete experience at all to draw from, the words only represent a group of letters. It brings no picture at all to mind.

Therefore, all communication between humans is interpretational. I know what I want to communicate. It is crystal clear to me. It just gets lost somewhere in the translation/interpretation. Many factors play a role in this basic miscommunication, including the lack of common experiences, the use of slang, different common experiences of the environment where you live, TV shows you watch, and games you play. They all result in the same word having different meanings to different people. It also includes what is not said or written. This includes reading between the lines and understanding hidden meanings.

What is not said or written or is omitted is also crucially important to interpret for effective communication to take place. Cultural understandings play a role in that certain body language, eye movement and location, tonality, dress, order, emphasis, words, and topics that cannot be clearly understood without knowing the context (culture) of the speaker or writer. To know something about the experiences of the speaker or writer helps communication be more effective.

Speaking is perhaps the most common form of communication and involves attempting "to communicate some particular idea, thought, or feeling to someone else verbally." Not only does the speaker get to use words, he also gets to use nonverbals like tonality, body language, pauses, eye contact, and, of course, what is not said by omission. These extra cues are frequently more meaningful than the actual words being spoken. They tell the story, provide context, and give added depth to the words being spoken.

The listener plays a huge role if effective communication is to take place. He must interpret what the speaker is attempting to communicate. He must ask questions, clarify, empathize, add facts and information, share definitions and perceptions, and provide support for the listener if what is to be communicated is done so effectively. Active listening is essential for deep understanding.

Writing is like speaking, except, instead of spoken words, symbols (letters, words, periods, commas, and so forth) are used. The reader does not have access to the writer's nonverbals. This makes effective communication more difficult because the reader must provide the context himself. The benefit of writing is that the writer has more time to make selections that will most accurately reflect what he is trying to communicate. Speaking is much more immediate so there is a greater chance to use words without careful consideration.

Communicating effectively also requires the speaker or writer to understand the context of the listener or reader. Purpose, audience, detail, depth, and the choice of which pattern to be used must all be taken into consideration. Each variable plays a role in how and what needs to be communicated. Without this type of understanding, miscommunication is the norm. The ability to utilize different forms of communication greatly enhances the ability to communicate effectively under differing circumstances and places the power of effective communication in the hands of the students. This is real power.

In most schools today, the language arts curriculum focuses on reading first and then writing. Learning to read is not about whole language, basals, phonics, or even phonemic awareness. These are strategies. Reading is about communicating a human experience, attempting to make meaning of alphabetic symbols. For young children, it must be connected to the concrete because they have relatively few experiences to draw upon. Remember, symbols are abstract representations and, in and of themselves, have little or no meaning.

These representations must therefore be experiential-based if students are to make the connection between real and abstract. Time and effort must be spent on questions such as:

- What do you think this word means?
- What experience does this word bring to mind?
- What colors, feelings, tastes, sensations, and emotions are connected to this item or experience?

Learning to spell fifty words correctly without meaning associated with each word is a waste of time because the words have no context.

In order to teach students effective communication skills, underlying thoughts and ideas must be brought to the surface. First and foremost is the understanding that all words are representations of a pattern. Years ago, I had the good fortune to speak at length with a Disney award–winning teacher from inner-city Chicago. I was curious as to what set her apart from her peers and asked her to explain how she taught in her classroom.

She first told me about her students. Forty-five first graders, half who spoke English as a second language. She told me about understanding that, without the concrete first, the symbols of the alphabet and therefore reading was impossible. So that's where she started.

"For example," she said, "when I teach the letter P, everything I can think of involves the letter itself. We eat, taste, and smell pancakes, plums, and popcorn. We wear pajamas. We paint with purples and pinks, and we smell perfumes." She would spend an entire week on one letter, and she provided context for the abstract symbol P.

She was right and, in my opinion, deserved the award because she made the abstract concrete for her students. She provided them with enough concrete experiences that the letters and words had meaning. They had tastes, smells, textures, and feelings so that, when they saw the letters PANCAKE, they represented something for which they had some knowledge.

Reading does not start with letters or even the alphabet. Reading starts with enough experiences so the patterns emerge for the learners. From these concrete patterns, students begin to realize that these representations, words, sentences, paragraphs, and stories communicate what is in their head and heart to others around them.

The teacher's role is to provide enough appropriate experiences so students see the connections. He must carefully select appropriate content, content that is developmentally appropriate, and that is interesting to the students (meets their needs today) (Glasser 2001). He must also provide students with options of words, language, and formats so effective communication is a result of choice. The ability to effectively express your experiences places the power of communication in the hands of the learner.

If teachers take on this task, all language arts teaching must be about expression of the human experience with words. They must say it, mean it, assess it, and grow it. It's the purpose, the point of the entire exercise. Everything the teacher and students do must be directly aligned with this purpose. If a learning activity does not directly enhance the student's ability to express his experiences with words (speaking, listening, writing, or reading), then the question must be asked, "Why am I teaching this stuff?" From the student's perspective, the question is, "Why do I have to know this stuff?"

# Chapter 7

# The Purpose of Social Studies

The study of social studies is not about white male generals, presidents, or famous explorers (someone else's hero). It's not about eras, geography, important dates, wars, and laws. When taught in isolation (without context), these topics and facts are irrelevant unless you happen to like the topic being studied. Historical facts and events have resulted when individuals, either alone or in social groups, have made choices in a certain context. Because of the ensuing consequences from those choices, they have been deemed worthy of notice. Human history provides a context for the important stuff that students want and need to learn about themselves and their role as social beings.

The content area purpose for teaching social studies is the human experience. Social studies addresses most directly what it means to be human for that individual at that time and place. This includes ideas such as time, place, power, conflict, and self-knowledge. The study of social studies is ultimately about questions that students have, either about themselves or how they are supposed to interact with others.

Internal or intrapersonal questions are the first level of questions that the majority of students are able to ask. This is normal from a maturity perspective in that children are growing from dependence to independence on the maturity continuum. They frequently ask the following types of questions:

- Why am I the way I am? Who am I?
- Is what I am feeling normal? Do others feel like this?
- Why don't I fit in? How do I fit in?
- What would I be like if I lived somewhere else or in a different time period?

- What would I be like if I had different parents?
- What would I be like if I had more money? Less money?
- What would I be like if I were more attractive? More athletic? More popular?
- What would I be like if I had more power?
- What do I want to be when I grow up?
- What makes me happy?
- What is life about anyway?
- What is my life's work?
- Who are my heroes? What does that tell me about myself?
- What/Who do I want to be when I grow up? (self-actualized issues)

External or interpersonal questions follow. They come when students begin to wonder about their role within groups and their relationships with other people. They are thinking about the move from independence to interdependence and have some of the following types of questions:

- What is expected of me as a son, daughter, friend, team member, and so forth?
- What responsibilities come with greater expectations?
- How do external expectations mesh with my need for independence?
- What roles am I expected to fill?
- Does society and family have the right to burden me with those expectations? What unwritten rules am I expected to follow? Whose rules are they anyway?
- What rites of passage do I need to undergo?
- How do I need to interact with others?
- When and under what conditions should I stand my ground or give in?
- How will I find out what groups and activities to participate in?
- Which clichés might I join: band, clubs, gangs, or athletics? What's my fit?
- What human connections do I need?
- When I change and grow, how does that affect my roles, interests, life, and past experiences?
- How do my changes affect others?
- How do I deal with all the feelings I have toward others? My love for friends and family? My sexual relationships?
- When are feelings unconditional and conditional?
- How do I need to deal with conflict, arguments, despair, and frustration in relationship to others?
- How do I deal with successes, accomplishments, and celebrations?

- When and under what conditions am I ready for life's transitions? How will I know? Do I have any control?
- Where does power come from?
- Who writes the rules? Where do unwritten rules come from? How do you change the rules? What is the point of the rules?
- When is freedom free? How is freedom tied to responsibility?

These questions are real for our students and are therefore emotion-laden. If what you are teaching is not emotion-laden, then it's the wrong issue to be teaching at that time.

My favorite group of students to work with was sophomores in high school. The issues that stressed them the most were exactly the issues I liked to talk and ask about and try to make them laugh about. These issues included learning to drive and its sense of increased power, dating (because parents no longer had to drive), independence, learning mistakes and their consequences and punishments, drinking, drugs, and sex. While I was their science teacher, these social studies topics were what they were concerned about on a daily basis. Failure to directly address these issues got in the way of learning in all their classes.

These interpersonal questions help us define who we are and how we interact with others. Therefore, the human experience is about addressing human issues that students have right now today. A deep understanding of human experiences might also reveal that all learning is egocentric. You learn what you choose to learn because it meets your needs and interests at that time and place. Learning is ultimately a personal experience. When you choose to learn something, that choice determines the amount of effort you put into the learning process.

Learning must be age and developmentally appropriate, which means you must ask the right question on the right topic at the right time or at the highest level. Design experiences so the students will ask the right question on the right topic at the right time. A rock-solid social studies curriculum is student-needs driven. The teacher must know his audience so well that he can address current student concerns directly. It is a human issue. Students must have the appropriate experiences and opportunities to grow from personal to group to culture to society to global perspective.

Because social studies deals with humans, the study of other humans is a useful strategy. Using individual people and knowing how they responded to the issues at hand and the consequences they experienced (the key point), allows connections to be made, and lessons can be learned from those previous experiences if students develop a relationship with the person being studied.

The consequences of those actions of others speak to the issue of options and choices, what was tried (and I had a connection with that person), and what happened. Therefore, their experience means this specific thing to me. This type of learning experience can only happen if the topic itself is relevant to the learner and the person being studied can generate a personal connection to the learner.

The teacher's role is a dual one: to select topics and questions that are relevant to the learner and to allow students the opportunity to have a personal connection to a person who has some learning experiences to share.

The second issue is a tough one for teachers tied to textbooks. What is required in terms of resources are primary sources, not sources that have been washed of all personal experiences. Students need to have stories told in the teller's own words. They need connections to be made between themselves and the people from the past, and they need to have the facts and feelings from someone they feel connected to.

These types of experiences are crucial so the students can draw their own conclusions. Resources therefore need to be experiential-based, such as diaries, artifacts (clothing, newspapers, music, instruments, and so forth), stories, field trips, reenactments, and trips to museums where they can touch things.

Learning experiences must provide opportunities that are concrete and have smells, tastes, textures, and emotions as part of the experience. Diaries work when the reader can make the personal connection between the writer and himself. Having everyone in a class read *The Diary of Anne Frank* misses the point entirely. Every student must have the opportunity to connect with someone on a personal level, and most eighth-grade boys find it difficult to make a personal connection to a fourteen-year-old girl who lived in a different country over fifty years ago.

Role-plays and stories also work very well to provide concrete experiences. Role-plays allow students the opportunity to visualize what it would be like to be someone else. They are required to think, act, and speak differently, so it provides them the opportunity to try on someone else's life (and choices and consequences).

The human learning experience is keenly attuned to stories, perhaps because of the importance of oral history in the past. People like stories and like to hear them more than once. In fact, good storytellers make the story come to life. Excellent stories most frequently have a moral or point that has a direct bearing on the listener. No matter how the experience is designed, the key is to make it as real as possible. The students must be able to see and feel that the actions were justifiable and experience the consequences of those actions.

To this end, it may also be said that one source is never enough for full and deep understanding. This means the core or deep patterns of what it means to be human have been exposed and addressed. One source is, in reality, just one way that the issue can be viewed. It is a for-that-person-at-that-time-and-at-that-place issue, and it is very easy to ignore the one, especially if there is no personal connection to the event or person being studied.

Human issues are also not just girl or boy issues, black or Native American or white issues, or poor or rich issues. They are human issues. Students must have access to multiple, diverse, concrete resources so the chances they will make a connection are increased. No connection means no deep understanding. The experiences provided must allow the students to answer questions such as:

- How did others in my position respond?
- What happened to them?
- What did they try?
- Did it work?
- What were the consequences of their decisions?

Most importantly, the questions are, "How can I apply that experience to me?" and "What can I learn from those experiences?"

The selection of content within this type of framework is crucial because it provides the foundation for all the learning experiences. The specific topic within the content to be taught must be relevant to the learners (addresses their questions and needs right then) and must have primary source availability (people, artifacts, role-plays, and so forth). The teacher must use the language (the human experience) on a daily basis if the students are to make the connections.

Finally, speaking to these human issues requires the ability to expresses those experiences effectively with words (language arts). Diversity issues are not issues you add on to your curriculum. Diversity is a requirement if students are to achieve deep understanding. Human issues rarely have one right answer. The ability to appreciate individuality within the group makes it easier for connections to be made, different perspectives to be validated, and generalizations to be robust and complex.

# Chapter 8

# The Purpose of Science

The study of science is not about memorization, covering the book, or identifying rocks, leaves, and insects. It's also not about dissecting things or hands-on activities that have one right answer (hands-on, brains-off). It is most certainly not about crossword puzzles, word finds, word scrambles, or even vocabulary lists. These tasks in and of themselves are not terrible. It's just that the isolated facts have no context. Real scientists do not sit around all day and memorize facts that are currently known. They do science, and that's what the students need to be doing as well.

The content area purpose for teaching science is problem-noticing to problem-solving. It is a process, a methodology for finding out that can be applied to many of life's problems.

When taught well, science helps students become more aware of their surroundings and be curious about what they are noticing. True science is action-oriented in that, not only must you be curious, you must also follow your curiosity to some sort of conclusion. Stating "A problem well stated is a problem half-solved" is a fundamental part of the finding-out process.

In life outside of schools, everyone has problems. The dilemma is that most people do not have a specific strategy or process for solving those problems effectively. Teaching students a methodology for noticing and solving problems helps them increase the odds of coming up with a good solution (there are no guarantees) in their personal lives outside the school setting.

A good solution may be defined as one that, in hindsight, the person could say, "At that time and at that place, knowing what I knew, I solved the problem as best I could." Students need the opportunity to practice these skills in all their science courses and in all grade levels. Problems never go away. They just change with age, development, and life's experiences. Doing science is the method by which content is addressed. As such, content becomes the platform for practicing these problem-noticing to problem-solving skills.

Science therefore attempts to teach a specific pattern of behavior that students can apply both in the classroom and their life outside of school. This pattern of behavior consists of the following steps:

## OBSERVATION

This is a teachable and learnable skill in that students must learn to break the bounds of normal observation. They must become consciously aware of their surroundings (people, places, and things). This is crucial because, once a pattern is established, a person becomes virtually oblivious to the smaller, more specific details.

A classic example is driving to work all the time and noticing a specific house for the first time. You know it is not new, and yet you never noticed it until today. Our brains put common experiences with previous similar experiences, and those habits must be broken if students are to grapple with fundamental problems and solutions.

Noticing skills include things like colors, textures, feelings, effects, relationships, smells, uses, size, and weight. Noticing skills also validates previous experiences and knowledge with the thing being noticed. Stories, uses, physical properties, and what it is like and not like all count as important information about the item or event. What you already know does in fact matter.

For this type of skill, working with others is a huge benefit. When a person notices something by himself, he has a tendency to notice only certain things. Some notice color, some textures, and some smells. Some are big into relationships or values. When we notice together, I have mine, and you have yours. Together, we notice more than we usually do alone. We all begin the process with more information than we would have had by ourselves, and this is good because you cannot wonder about something of which you are unaware.

## CURIOSITY

With lots of new information about their surroundings or specific material related to the topic of study at hand, students must then be asked to be curious. What is it about the things they have noticed that makes them say, "I wonder …" This is really a key point to the entire process and the one that is most frequently not emphasized or taught.

Curiosity sets up the learning journey because it is emotion-laden (an ownership issue) in that it is a question the individual has framed for himself in his mind. Curiosity is also where imagination comes to life because it questions the way things currently are and imagines what might be. Outside-the-box thinking needs to be the norm for this step in the process. When people continue to do what has always been done before, it is a clear sign that curiosity is dormant.

Good teachers also have the ability to help the students question the reality they have noticed from shallow to complex levels. Helping students to wonder about colors, shapes, and textures and pushing them to wonder about more complex patterns and relationships that might exist requires an enormous depth of content knowledge on the part of the teacher. All students can be helped to become more curious about their world and wonder about why things exist as they do. Good teachers can make it happen.

## STATEMENT OF THE PROBLEM

Curiosity is a wonderful thing and makes even the common extraordinary. It sets up the next step because, while curiosity is essential, it is also not action-oriented. You can be the most curious person alive and yet accomplish or solve nothing. Curiosity needs to go farther. That is where the next step, statement of the problem, becomes essential.

Putting action to curiosity requires that students learn to set goals for what they would really like to find out, solve, or prove. The two formats that follow help provide a simple structure to help students put action to their curiosity:

- The problem is (action word): What they are curious about
- In what ways can we (action word): What they are curious about

Action words specify the goal or objective the students have set for themselves. Setting out to find out, prove, or solve what they are curious about helps them learn to be in charge of their own learning.

## GATHERING INFORMATION

Once the goal has been set, it becomes important to find out what is already known. This is one of the two major areas where content becomes a crucial piece in the process. The information the students gathers sets the background for the rest of the learning to come.

Textbooks, encyclopedias, magazines and journals, experts in the field, and Internet sources can all provide information that might possibly help the students meet their learning goals and objectives. This research continues to help them clarify what they want to know and focus their efforts toward solving, proving, or finding out about.

A key point that needs to be emphasized here is that, since the observation step, the entire process has been abstract. What follows is the concrete expression of what they think they know.

## HYPOTHESIS FORMATION

In order to make the process concrete and continue to provide ownership for the students, they must now make an educated guess about what they believe to be true. It is educated because they have already gathered relevant information about the process in question.

Hypotheses are prediction-based. You make a guess and then try to prove if your guess was accurate. They are beautiful in that, no matter if your guess was accurate or not, you now know more than you did before. It is always a learningful experience and ultimately one that asks more questions than it answers. Hypotheses set the stage for finding out for sure in the form of what are you going to test.

## EXPERIMENTATION

Let's play! Let's test and try to experiment and find out for ourselves what really happens. It doesn't matter if the teacher already knows the answer. It also doesn't even really matter if the world knows the answer. To the student, experimentation is the process of making the abstract information real and concrete for himself.

To this end, it is crucially important that students learn specific experimental design considerations; otherwise, they can have no confidence in what they found out. They must learn to design experiments that have controlled, dependent, and independent variables and know what they all mean.

The word "experiment" itself sets the stage for learning. To experiment means that the results are unknown. Therefore, most school science experiments are not. Teachers need to call them lab activities because, as soon as there is one expected answer that the teacher can grade, it is in no way an experiment. It is certainly hands-on, but it is also certainly brains-off.

Students have no input into what they want to find out when they just follow the directions step-by-step. The context has been lost.

After designing the experiment, the students must then do the experiment! They must carry out their test and gather the data that results.

## DATA ANALYSIS

After the completion of the experiments, students now have some facts or data, but what do they mean? Now comes the time to put your data and information together in a way that makes it clear what really happened.

Analysis is required. Depending on the type of experiment that was done, statistical analysis may be called for. Data tables and charts help organize the data and graphically represent what happened during the experiment itself. What the data tells you and what it tells you about your hypothesis are critical factors for good data analysis.

## CONCLUSION

So your guess was either supported or rejected. That's nice, but not really the main point. The main point is, "What did I learn?" The conclusion is the second place where content places a crucial role in that it is the explanation of why what happened in the experiment happened. It is not about excuses (bad experimental design or technique). It is the content explanation for the results that were recorded. You made a guess, and you tested it and found out some stuff. What does it really mean? That is the essence of the conclusion. Good conclusions are always content-rich and finally set the stage for what's next. Here is an example of how the process might look in life outside of schools:

Let's say I own a 1989 Plymouth Caravan. One day on the way to work, I have to pick up a friend whose car is broken. When I pick him up, he asks me about the oil smell and funny noises it makes when it shifts. I hadn't really noticed, but, because he mentioned it, it does smell like it's burning oil. So that's what that cloud following me is. It really does make funny noises when it shifts. I begin to wonder what's going on. Does it need to get fixed? Is it time for a new car? How much longer can I nurse it along? Am I going to make it home tonight after school?

I state the problem. The problem is finding out how much it will cost to fix my car. I make an appointment with a mechanic and ask him to look over the car, especially the smoke and noises when it shifts. I ask him to give me an estimate of repair and if he believes it is worth fixing (gathering information). He calls me at school and tells me not to bother. Repairs will cost more than the car is worth.

I must now rethink the issue (curiosity): nurse it along or look for other options. I decide and restate the problem. The problem is finding a new car (to me). I begin to look around, ask my friends about what they own and how they like it, look in *Car and Driver* and *Consumer Report*, and begin to formulate a picture of the kind of vehicle I think I might want. I might even call my insurance agent and ask about the cost of insuring different vehicles. Finally, I narrow my choices (hypothesis formation) and decide I am going to look at two or three specific models.

I go to the some auto dealers and take some test drives (experimentation). I might even take them home and let the family share the experience with me. I ask for the specific deals for each and perhaps even get each of the deals in writing. I go home, sit down with the family, and analyze our experiences of driving feel and smell, color, options, cost, insurance, and so forth (data analysis). Finally, we pick one, call the dealer, and make the deal (conclusion).

Science is ultimately about making the abstract concrete for our learners. It is about being proactive, and it provides students a pattern for noticing and then solving problems that exist in their lives today right now.

Finally, let it also be said that there are things in this life that are okay to test and experiment with for yourself. There are other things where the risk may be too high. Safety issues, drugs, cheating, stealing, drinking and driving, and sex probably fall in the high-risk category. As adults, we may wish to tell our students not to do something, hoping to save them from making big mistakes. Frequently, we learned about those issues from making those mistakes ourselves, but, in reality, we are asking students to trust us on this issue.

As adults, we have to use our trust card very carefully. If we use it for trivial things and they experiment and find out that what we said really doesn't happen, the amount of trust placed in our advice diminishes. We lose power. For example, you could say that throwing a snowball may knock out someone's eye. When they do and it doesn't, that now opens them to ask the question, "What else can't I trust them about?"

When students learn the scientific pattern or process and come to trust the information they gather, perhaps they will not have to depend upon their own experiences with quite as much conviction. Teachers must tie the scientific process to human problems with them and their need for relevance.

At deepest levels, this becomes relatively simple to do if the artificial separation between all the content areas is overcome. Focusing on major themes that exist in all science fields also reveals human themes. For example, cycles (things with no real beginnings or ends) also represents patterns that exist among humans (child, adolescent, adult, and aged). Classification is about relationships, and work, power, and energy are common terms among many fields with human implications as well. Physical and chemical change surrounds us every day and every way. Structure and function deals not just with anatomy, but with systems we are part of as well. It is all connected at the deepest levels.

# Chapter 9

# The Purpose of Mathematics

The study of mathematics is not about memorizing math facts or even adding, subtracting, multiplying, or dividing. It's not about memorizing theorems and solving proofs. It's not even about getting ready for the next math class in the sequence. It's also not about algebra, geometry, advanced math, or, horror of horrors, even calculus. When mathematics is taught with the focus only on the isolated facts, it lacks context and any connection to students' lives outside of school.

The content area purpose of mathematics is to notice and explain patterns using symbols. It is an analysis and relationship activity and is ultimately prediction-based.

The human brain is an organ and, as such, performs specific tasks. In terms of learning, the human brain might be classified as a pattern-seeking organ. It looks for patterns among things and tries to see what the relationships are between the pieces. The brain also has the ability to do this in a very messy (non-sequential) world. For example, let us go back to the concept of "dog-ness."

Children do not learn this concept in one day. Most parents, although there might be some, do not schedule an entire day with dogs of all sorts of colors, shapes, and sizes to help their child learn the word "dog." Children might see a dog every now and then. To which, the parent points and says the word "dog" or even "doggie" very slowly. This happens over and over again. When the child begins to say the word "dog," he will frequently be pointing at a cat, cow, horse, or perhaps even a mouse.

Each of the incorrectly identified animals had hair, four legs, ears, and eyes. The differences can be very subtle. It takes lots of practice to connect the correct word with a specific pattern that exists. Each individual word represents a very specific pattern. For the most part, humans can do this relatively easily.

Generally speaking, humans like patterns. In many cases, we function by our patterns. Other names for patterns are habits, routines, or schedules. We like them because they are predictive in nature. If we know the pattern, we can explain it, describe it, and make decisions based on it. In reality, each prediction and ensuing result based on that prediction helps us clarify the pattern in more detail.

Mathematics chooses not to use words to describe particular patterns that exist. They use an entirely different set of symbols such as numbers, functions, and other representations. Mathematics also attempts to explain the relationship between the pieces of the pattern. For example, $2 + 3 = 5$ has five different symbols and explains the relationship between the items. Changing any one item changes the entire pattern and representation.

Just as words (a combination of letters) represent items, behaviors, things, ideas, and thoughts and are best learned through concrete experiences, mathematic symbols represent things as well. Representations are just what it says. They are representations, not the real thing, and they are abstractions. They can be very useful, but, for the huge majority of learners, they must be based on multiple, diverse, concrete experiences so the learner realizes what is being represented. The understanding of any representation must be based on experiences.

In mathematics, patterns have special names: formulas, functions, numbers, equations, and, perhaps the most important of all, relationships. Simple patterns can be represented with simple symbols and relationships. $2 + 3 = 5$ is an example of simple symbols (numbers) and simple relationships (adding and equivalence).

As patterns become more complex, simple symbols are no longer sufficient to describe them and are therefore replaced with other, more abstract symbols. Arithmetic basically speaks to patterns that can be represented through the use of numbers. Generally speaking, most people have learned all the arithmetic they need to function in life by the end of sixth grade.

Algebra begins the study of more complex patterns and the relationship between the pieces. For example, let us consider the following allowance example:

Imagine you are fifteen years old and want an increase in your allowance from your parents. You know right off the bat that you have to ask your dad because your mom is tight with the cash. You also realize you have to ask your dad at the right time, after payday before the bills have been paid and early in the morning because he's tired and grouchy when he gets home. You also know he's more likely to say yes to anything after you have buttered him up by asking his advice, making him laugh, or giving him a few compliments.

Each of these factors could be represented by a symbol. The relationship could be described with an equation:

- $X$ = Getting an increase in allowance
- $A$ = Dad
- $B$ = Time of Day
- $C$ = Day of Month
- $D$ = Mood of Dad

$X = A + B + C + D$. So you plan your strategy carefully, taking all the variables into account. You feel pretty confident as you put your plan into action. You wake up early on the day after payday, make your dad coffee, and give him a big hug, telling him how he is the best dad in the world. He smiles, and you smile and ask for the increase.

He looks sad and tells you he would love to, but his hours at work have been cut. In fact, you will have to take a decrease in the next three month's allowance. Nice try, but new variables of which you were unaware have emerged. The pattern has to be reevaluated.

If life consists of patterns and our brain is a pattern-seeking organ, then it should be possible to represent those patterns using symbols and use them to make better predictions. Stories, science experiments, teams, houses, cars, sandwiches, and problems are all fair game for mathematics. If it is a pattern, we should be able to describe it with symbols. And if that is true, then we should be able to tie mathematics to the lives of our students, every day and in every way.

There are some obvious problems with the way mathematics is currently taught. One of the most grievous errors is the premature move from concrete items and patterns to abstract representations, which happens way too early developmentally. Just as in the Montana dog story, students must be helped to understand the pattern at a deep level before they move on to the representations of those patterns.

Another problem with how mathematics is currently taught is that many mathematics teachers do not themselves know what patterns the formulas and symbols represent. If you don't believe this, then ask ten math teachers what pattern from life outside the school setting is represented by $A = B + C$. Ask them each for ten examples, and see how many can answer the question. (A represents anything that is made up of only two pieces, like a couple.) The inability to answer this question is the crux of the matter. Without the ability to transfer the representation to reality (concretization), students see them only as formulas that have absolutely no relevance to everyday life.

The inability to see the patterns that the symbols represent also leads to giving students answers to "Why do I have to know this?" that are perhaps on the intrinsically unmotivating side of things. Answers frequently given sound like, "You have to know this stuff for the next chapter, the next course, the math course next year, or your college math course." Once arithmetic has been taught, most students see little relevance for mathematics. And if it were not required, they would probably not take much math after sixth grade.

Even in arithmetic, the lack of pattern recognition plays a teaching and learning role. For example, let's take a quick look at the teaching of math facts: adding, subtracting, multiplying, and dividing. Many teachers and school districts teach each set of facts as isolated entities. They are not related. So a student must learn one hundred individual facts for each function, adding, subtracting, multiplying, and dividing.

At the shallowest level of understanding, the adding facts can be reduced to forty items very easily: twos, threes, fives, and sevens. There is no need to memorize fours because they are every other two. Sixes are either every third two or every other three. Eights are every fourth two or every other four. Nines are every third three. Sixty isolated facts could be eliminated, and that time includes the amount spent on understanding what pattern adding really represents.

At the next level of understanding, some of the functions begin to be seen as being related and are just different ways of grouping. Multiplying is just fast adding (shorthand) because three times six means three groups of six or six groups of three ($6 + 6 + 6$ or $3 + 3 + 3 + 3 + 3 + 3$). Dividing is just fast subtracting. Twenty-one divided by seven really means how many groups of seven are in twenty-one items ($21 - 7 - 7 - 7$). At the deepest level of understanding, numbers are taught as representations for a quantity of something. So it is only necessary to teach eleven concepts and all the variations that make them up ($0$–$10$).

It is all grouping. We as humans work with different groupings every day. In fact, it is not unusual for even young children to know how to count by nines, elevens, eights, fives, threes, and fours. Nines are used in baseball, as are threes and fours. Football and soccer require counting by elevens. Music uses eights, and basketball uses fives, ones, twos, and threes. People group in many more ways than just in tens. This is crucial to understand when students are asked to learn double digits. In fact, if they do not understand grouping well, they can divide, but will have no idea what it really means.

When taught with a depth of understanding in mind, students will learn and understand the math facts and the relationships between the functions. In the long run, time would be saved because not every teacher would have to reteach the math facts over and over and over again. Students might even come to realize the importance of mathematics to their daily lives.

# Chapter 10

# The Purpose of Health and Physical Education

The study of health and physical education is not about dodgeball, basketball, volleyball, or any other ball or game. It is also not about scaring kids straight, always doing what an adult tells you to do, or learning about your body in a way that is way too little and too late. Lastly, it is not about growing up as a function of luck, figuring out things like drinking, sex, and drugs on your own from your friends, just like your mom and dad learned it.

The content area purpose of health and physical education is decision-making and the strategies by which good decisions are made. A good decision may be defined as the following, "At that time and at that place, knowing what I knew, I made a decision that I thought was going to work." Most frequently, humans do not wake up one morning and say, "Today, I am going to make some decisions that will haunt me for the rest of my life." It just happens, and it happens more frequently when decisions are made haphazardly and without thought or process. There has to be a different way to learn decision-making rather than trial and error, and health and physical education is designed to meet that need.

The beauty of physical education, exercise, and games is that the consequences of decisions made can be seen and felt very quickly. When involved in a game, the bad pass or poor decision is seen right away and has an immediate consequence. This allows many teachable moments to be addressed within any one game.

The question that arises immediately after some action is, "What were you considering when you made that choice or decision?" Students are allowed the opportunity to see and feel the connection between choices and consequences in a safe environment, where making an errant pass might cause the game to tip, but is not a matter of life and death. They are allowed the opportunity to practice their decision-making skills and develop confidence in their abilities.

Some health topics allow students the same opportunity to see consequences, but most require a longer time lapse between the decision and the consequence. Beginning to exercise has about a three-week time lag between starting and seeing the effects of the exercise. Eating a healthier diet may take even longer to see the effects. For smoking, drugs, and alcohol, we want them to trust their own ability to make solid decisions without concrete experiences at all.

When students are helped to learn that solid decisions require thought and are criteria-based, decision-making processes can become a habit. This, of course, has lifelong implications. Wellness issues all revolve around decisions that a person makes, such as eating (what, when, and how much), sleeping (how much is enough), and exercise (what kind, how much, and for what purpose). These are, of course, tied to developmental issues as well and the right-amount-at-the-right-time concept. Quality of life decisions can be discussed as opportunities to practice decision-making skills before the student tries them on his own first.

Questions relating to sex (when, with whom, and why), dealing with peer pressure, and self-esteem can all be discussed within the framework of criteria and consequences of each decision that is made. Adults are not present when children make the most important decisions of their lives. We are not there when they have to decide about drinking. We are not there when they have to decide about sex. We are not there when they have to decide about drugs. If we cannot be there to save them, then we should at least provide them with the tools they need to make a good decision.

Therefore, health and physical education is about safety net issues. This means helping students to realize that every decision, even doing nothing, has a consequence. If a student wishes to make a decision that goes against the norm for that situation, support mechanisms are in place to support him.

In my younger years, I coached two different sports in high school. Every semester or when the need arose, the coaches would get together to discuss students who had broken the athletic code of conduct. This code basically forbade drinking, drugs, and doing poorly in school. Students who had broken the code had to suffer certain consequences. For first-time infractions, the course of action was frequently probation or sometimes double-secret probation à la *Animal House*. We as coaches thought it was a relatively good system and had the support of many parents and most of the students.

Driving home from an away tennis meet one day, I got into a serious discussion with some of the girls who informed me that they actually enjoyed being on probation. This was hard for me to understand. How could a punishment be enjoyed? That, of course, was the conversation.

When a student athlete was on probation and then went to a party, all he had to say when someone offered him a beer or some pot was, "You know I'm on probation. If I get caught again, I will get kicked off the team." Most frequently, that ended the peer pressure. In fact, for some athletes, other peers would in fact not even allow drinks and such to be offered. Being on probation actually made it easier to stand by unpopular decisions!

The same thinking about safety nets can be applied to other students and children. If the child knows the parent is going to be waiting up and checking, especially if his friends know the parents as well, he has an easy out. "You know my dad is going to be waiting at the front door for me when I get home." This is a safety net. It allows the burden to be placed onto the adult to make a tough decision easier. If, of course, the child wants to drink, smoke, and so forth, waiting by the door will not change that behavior!

The ability to make good decisions also requires the tools to make it happen. There is never just one right answer. It always depends. It is a dynamic process with many variables, and it changes depending on the people present, the place, and the need for the decision. Consistently making good decisions requires a type of balance within a changing context (your life).

Good decisions require information, the right amount at the right time, and a method or process to follow (pros and cons, idea evaluators, and lists) so decisions are made thoughtfully and are prediction-based. Decisions must be made by the individual himself with little or no adult or peer pressure to skew the thinking process. This is the fine point because novices do not know the criteria for effective decision-making within that specific context while experts do know the criteria. In fact, knowing the appropriate criteria is the hallmark for an expert. Experts notice and know different things that novices do not.

When I was much younger, I used to run on a regular basis and enjoyed the vacation of the mind that the exercise used to provide. Unfortunately, I began to experience some physical problems, and my left leg began to tingle and go numb. I tried unsuccessfully to fix it and ultimately decided a new form of exercise was called for.

I finally decided on bicycle riding, but had no bike and didn't really know what kind or model to buy. At that time, a student in one of my classes was very into bike riding and racing. In fact, he later went to college on a bicycle riding scholarship. I gave him my parameters ($300) and told him what I wanted to do with the bike. I asked him to pick one out for me.

He was very excited and went out shopping to this shop and that shop. He came and talked about what he was learning. He asked more specific questions about the type of riding I was thinking about doing. After about two to three weeks, he came in and told me his choice.

I, of course, asked what made that specific model and brand the one for me (the criteria). He carefully explained about the gears and the weight, reliability factors of the brand, and how this particular bike met the requirements I had set forth. He was outlining the criteria he (the expert) had considered before making the choice. I did in fact buy that specific bike. As a matter of fact, I still have it and ride it regularly. It has been a great bike for me!

Sharing the appropriate criteria without giving specific advice is crucial to the learning experience. It provides for the flow of information and yet allows the choice to remain with the individual. Criteria also change with circumstances and goals. If I had been interested in road racing, the criteria would have been very different.

Sharing of expert criteria versus telling someone what to do or pick allows people to see others as experts and perhaps even mentors. They are more willing to listen and perhaps learn something for themselves from the choices made and the ensuing consequences of others.

There is a right way and time to learn from experiences. Not all experiences lead to learning. Have you ever made the same mistake over and over again? If so, you have clearly not learned (changed your behavior) due to some prior experience. To learn from an experience means to reflect upon the choices you made and the ensuing consequences and change your behavior the next time you are in that position. It requires you to reconsider your thinking process, the criteria you used to make the choice, and what was not considered that might have played a major role.

The best time to learn from an experience is when it is still emotion-laden, but not so much that thinking is limited. These teachable moments mean the individual is ready for long-term learning. Emotion is perhaps the major gate from short- to long-term memory. It is why we can so vividly remember our most embarrassing moments. The emotion carries the experience virtually uncensored from short- to long-term memory.

When the learner is ready emotionally, criteria become evident in that what was not considered has changed the expected outcome and can reinforce those criteria that were considered. The clear and powerful consequences are being felt by the learner right then and there.

Saving children repeatedly from the consequences of their actions keeps them from powerful learning opportunities. Taking advantage of teachable moments is the key to effective teaching and learning. Master teachers can in fact design learning experiences where teachable moments are planned.

A climate where the norm is learning from experience requires an orientation between the students and the teacher. The teacher must precariously balance the opportunity to learn with safety and harm issues. Young children must be provided opportunities to make decisions with small consequences for failure. If they have matured in making decisions, older kids must be provided opportunities for decisions with larger consequences.

A consequence is a natural result related to the action taken. For example, if you break a plate, the consequence of that action would be to clean it up and replace the plate. A punishment is a result not aligned with the action taken. For example, if you break a plate, you sit in the corner, get yelled at, and perhaps even get a spanking. Different lessons are learned from consequences and punishment. Punishment most frequently provides the learning for lack of trust in the adult and making sure not to get caught the next time. Consequences provide learning opportunities for making better decisions the next time.

With this decision-making orientation in mind, games take on a whole new orientation. They become options for recreation as well as options for fitness. They provide immediate consequences for decisions and teachable moments in abundance. When activities are structured with this in mind, rules themselves begin to be viewed as tools versus only as limits.

## SANDLOT GAMES

In the old days when I was growing up, kids from the neighborhood would get together to play some games without any adults to tell us what to do. One of the games we used to play was baseball. The dilemma was that we never had eighteen players (nine on a side) or a real field. Besides which, we had kids of all different ages and ability levels: novices, experts, and really young kids to old kids. But we all wanted to play baseball and have fun.

So we had to make up our own rules. Pitcher's Hand was one variation, because you didn't need to have a first baseman. Other rules were that, when teams were chosen, the person who picked second got to have two picks right away to compensate for not getting the best player with the number-one pick. Right field was either a foul ball or an out. Some people had to bat opposite-handed. Ghost runners were part of most every game, and you sometimes had to field opposite-handed to give the batter an extra chance.

The people who played had to make rules that kept the game fun. Not only that, there had to be general consensus to follow the rules because, if you didn't like the rules, you could always take your ball and go home. You also had to enforce the rules because there were no umpires. You had to make all the calls yourself. These were powerful learning experiences for all the kids involved.

We began to understand that people make rules, and they are to help define the game and keep things fair. Rules can change depending on the situation.

One set of rules can work fine, but, if even only a few people leave, the rules have to change because everything else has changed. You also have to agree to follow the rules, and there has to be general agreement on how to enforce them. We learned when to fight and when to let it go. This was powerful learning indeed.

Therefore, what we have to learn to understand is that rules have a purpose. They define the pattern of the game. They need to be fair if you want to keep everyone involved. As life changes for the individual and society, so should your rules. Humans made them; humans can change them. Rules are power. Whoever makes and monitors the rules has the power. And by the way, another name for rules is criteria. Without these types of experiences, deep understanding on the part of the students is wishful thinking.

# Chapter 11

# The Purpose of Art

The study of art is not about coloring, especially inside the lines, or memorizing famous artists and their works. It's for sure not about cutting out pumpkins, turkeys, or snowmen depending on the season. It is also, at the deepest level, not about painting, drawing, or sculpting well. Art goes much deeper. It's not that any of these activities are not worth doing, but, without the context (purpose), opportunities for learning are missed.

The content area purpose of art is expressing the human experience through two- and three-dimensional representations. It is fundamentally a representational activity where some object represents something in particular from within the artist.

Art is therefore an expression of the inner being and fundamentally cannot be represented by words. The artwork itself is not the feeling, thought, idea, or whatever else is inside the artist. Artwork represents the feeling, thought, idea, or whatever else the artist is trying to express at that point in time. Art is dependent upon the skills of the artist and is an extension of the experiences, perspective, mood, and need to communicate on the part of the artist.

Creating art and viewing art are twin functions, just like speaking and listening or writing and reading. For the person viewing the art, it becomes an interpretational activity for him in that it requires the viewer to search deeply inside himself to see what feelings are being moved, what thoughts are being stirred, and what ideas are being created. Art is much more abstract than speaking and writing in that only one object has to communicate it all. The object must represent the entire communication.

Art is therefore, by its very nature, beyond words. It is art. It speaks to life, feelings, beliefs, thoughts, and perspectives. "A picture is worth a thousand words" is exactly the point. It may or may not have a purpose to the viewer, but art always has a point to the artist.

For our students, art is an outlet for what is deep inside that cannot be expressed with words. They need opportunities to play with those thoughts, ideas, and feelings and represent them directly and concretely. They need opportunities to draw, paint, do ceramics, sculpt, photograph, make jewelry, and play with design. Each type of art calls on different strengths and forms of representation and allows the students the opportunity to see which works best for them. They must have the opportunity to learn the skills that allow them to communicate without words most effectively.

Creating art is also a heavily creative activity. Creativity can be defined as "putting pieces together that have not been put together before" (Davis 2004). Therefore, art, which is based on your experiences, skills, viewpoint, perspectives, beliefs, and feelings, is a creative exercise because you are unique. Art allows for new perspectives, combinations, and connections to be made on the part of the artist. In fact, if one hundred people were to do exactly the same art activity, each work would be different and unique. Some would be done better than others, and they would each be art.

At the deepest level, art is ageless and timeless. It has the ability to strike the inner chord of humans whoever they might be and close the gap between generations. It is like the statue of David, the *Mona Lisa*, or a house by Frank Lloyd Wright. It can be experienced over and over again and always touch that inner chord. It always speaks to the viewer in new and different ways. True art ultimately evokes emotion, either positive or negative. Like Picasso, you might love it or hate it, but it is virtually impossible to be indifferent.

The ability to see, feel, and realize what is inside and deal with them directly (represent them with art) allows people to be artists not just in art. Doing anything at the deepest level becomes art. Art becomes how you live your life, how you do your job, and who you are. Life itself becomes a work of art. You can tell who the artists are by how they talk, the words they use, the passion with which they live, and the joy of learning and doing that permeates their lives.

Art is not just for artists. Art is the way things are done. There are workers, craftsmen, and artisans who all do the same job, but how they do the job is fundamentally different. A worker gets the job done. A craftsman gets the job done well. An artisan makes the work into a piece of art. It has to do with harmony, the interconnectedness of the pieces, the detail, the depth, and the fit. The simplicity or the essence is obvious, and it strikes an inner chord. There are chairs. There is furniture. And then there is art.

# Chapter 12

# The Purpose of Music

The study of music is not about playing the piano, the trumpet, or the drums. It's not even about reading notes and all the symbols in a piece of music. It's also not about playing someone else's music alone or in a band/orchestra or singing in a choir. While learning to read music and play instruments is crucially important, at the deepest levels, it still misses the point (purpose).

The content area purpose of music is the expression of the human experience through sounds. Music communicates something about the human experience in a way that words cannot.

Music may be the most visceral communication experience. It literally pounds within humans in rhythm with the communication. We begin to synchronize with the music both physiologically and emotionally. Music can make us happy or sad or make us laugh or cry. It can get people ready for battle or sob brokenheartedly with the sheer tragedy of the story. Music is empathy without words. It is a story told in beats and rhythms; in loud, blaring noises; and the soft whisper of a single note. It connects humans in a way perhaps no other medium can.

Composing music and listening to music are twin functions similar to creating art and viewing art. For the composer, music is a dynamic interplay between each of the instruments being used and the rhythms, beats, volumes, pitches, silences, tones, and, most critically, the interplay between them all. It is literally the challenge of juggling one hundred balls at the same time in a dance to communicate a specific idea, thought, or feeling. For the listener, it is a question of interpretation, how effectively this particular piece of music strikes an inner resonance so a personal connection is achieved.

Music, like art, is a representational activity. It is not the feeling itself, nor the thought nor the story. Music speaks to each individual in a way that is beyond words. It is the stuff of humans, stories, emotions, wins and losses, opportunities lost and taken, birth and death, and the highest highs and lowest lows. Human experience enriches the music for both the composer and the listener.

In schools, music needs to be part of the everyday experience. Music is made up of patterns and sometimes patterns within patterns and can therefore provide concrete experiences for students to feel a specific pattern. This ability to concretize patterns is the basis for the close relationship between mathematics and music. The pattern can be so clear and powerful that it becomes easily represented.

Whole notes (numbers) and beats per measure (fractions) become obvious and provide young learners with multiple avenues to experience particular patterns and their representations. When done in groups, music also provides concrete experiences with interdependence issues. It is important that each individual does his particular job well, but it takes everyone working together, doing different jobs, and playing different instruments to make it really truly work. Every student needs these kinds of experiences and needs them every single school day.

While playing and singing music are powerful learning experiences, without the context of expressing human experience through sounds, the deepest level of learning achieved is that of playing or singing well. Students need the opportunities to make their own music and develop the skills to communicate effectively through sounds. They need opportunities to play and play with all sorts of instruments, those with strings and those of metal, those of wood and those you beat, and even those they make by themselves.

Each instrument has its own special form of communication, which can change from being played alone or with other instruments. Play can lead to harmonies discovered, an alignment between the music and the internal workings. It becomes the search for the right instrument or tool at the right time to exactly express the right thing. By its very nature, music is interrelationship-oriented. When done with a group, synergy (knowing more together than knowing as a collection of individuals) occurs as a natural outcome. Each piece plays its own part, but together music is made.

When composed, each musical piece has its own special purpose that the composer had in mind and therefore represents a feeling, story, thought, or belief and shares that experience from within the composer. When that musical piece is played, the conductor or musician interprets or makes the music as he hears it. The performance is his interpretation of the work and becomes tied to his own feelings, stories, thoughts, or beliefs from his personal experiences.

Listening to music has powerful, long-term effects. Songs become linked to times and experiences of our lives in deep and powerful ways. Hearing a song you have not heard for many years can move you deeply and make the emotions you felt then come back in full force. It is as if all the time in between has disappeared and you are back in the experience once more. Music has power.

## Chapter 13

# The Purpose of Vocational Education

The study of vocational education is not about courses for dummies or being a dumping ground for discipline problems or special education students who struggle in regular classrooms. It is also not about cooking and sewing for girls and welding and auto classes for boys. The fact is that having an entire content area devoted to this topic shows how fragmented education has become. The model for effective vocational education instruction needs to be at the heart of all public school teaching.

The content area purpose of vocational education courses is the application of theory to life skills. You take what you know or are learning and do something with it.

The vocational education model basically provides the application experiences in a real-world setting for everything they are supposed to be learning in school. Vocational education provides for the concretization of theory that developmentally makes sense for the learners. It is the difference between

- Writing a paper for a class versus writing an article for the community paper
- Giving a speech to the teacher and your classmates versus convincing the school board to change the school day
- Memorizing science facts or conducting a science experiment
- Learning fractions via worksheet or learning fractions by building something to scale

If what is to be learned has no application, then the point is what? The vocational education model is clear and simple. Learn about it, design and plan it, and then do it. And isn't that what life is about? The consequences for decisions made become more powerful because the learning is demonstrated through something concrete and real to those outside the school setting. This type of learning has many advantages. First and foremost is that the end product or vision for the learning is fairly obvious. This means that students know what they are striving for and the end product has a real-world audience.

Another advantage of this model is that the tasks are complex, which means that, in order to achieve an end result or vision of quality, multiple steps are required. Practice, reworking, more practice, and more reworking are also a natural part of the process. Failure, attempting something, and having it not work as expected is part of the learning process and provides for many teachable moments within the context of the task.

Homework is not seen as homework that the teacher expects, but as tasks that need to be completed so the next task can be completed. Assessments become meaningful because they are done both on a task-by-task level as well as on the final product.

Quality is clear and obvious and is determined by criteria, which were established at the very beginning of the learning experience, along with the vision itself. Student ownership of the end product makes the process real and meaningful and provides opportunities for authentic celebrations of learning for the students and those who support them.

Not only are celebrations of learning authentic, assessments can be equally as authentic. In fact, one of the best examples of rubrics I have ever seen was in a welding class.

On the teacher's desk were pieces of metal with varying qualities of welds. First were two pieces of metal not joined at all. The next one, the weld was not continuous. The third was welded but was not smooth and thinner and thicker in places. The fourth was a very nice weld, fairly even but not totally smooth. The fifth was a work of art. It connected the pieces of metal in a way that showed they were more than the individual pieces.

The real beauty of the rubric was that, when a student wanted to see how well he was doing, he would just go to the front of the room and compare his weld to the examples on the desk. He would move his weld from one example to the next and back again and finally either go back and practice some more or go find the teacher and ask for help. It was beautiful to see, and the power and independence of student learning was clear and evident.

The apprenticeship model used most frequently in vocational education can also provide for important connections between the community and schools. The embedded use of mentors and experts in the field helps students learn clear, real, and specific patterns of behavior and thought for the tasks they are attempting to learn while providing the experts and mentors an audience to share their expertise. Both parties learn and grow, and connections are made, which break down the walls of the school.

Unfortunately, this model of learning is used most generally with only those students who are labeled as non-college bound. Even more unfortunate is how they find themselves in that predicament. Tracking or ability grouping plays a major role in how a student might find himself in a vo-ed class or program. To state it as succinctly as possible, it is frequently a quality of life issue in regards to jobs and careers to which a student might aspire.

Ability grouping begins in first grade with the formation of reading groups. There are always three (Oakes 2005), even in gifted classes. Some teachers even go so far as to try to disguise the groups by assigning special names, like bluebirds, robins, and crows, but the children figure out which ability group they are in within the first ten minutes. Putting students into groups to learn is not the problem, but the differences in instruction that occur from group to group becomes a huge problem, at least for the boys. This way of grouping and the differences in instruction that result is most assuredly the most discriminatory practice that exists in schools today.

The problems begin with the makeup of the groups themselves. Clearly, not every child reads at the same level at the beginning of first grade. But for boys, it becomes a problem because the lowest and slowest reading group is almost always made up entirely of boys and, for the most part, boys who are also seen as discipline problems because they can't sit still. This is not to be unexpected because boys clearly lag developmentally behind girls.

Generally speaking, boys are potty trained later than girls, frequently up to one and a half years later, and play with their toys and peers very differently than girls do. Their small motor skill development lags behind girls to a significant degree. These are physiological differences and have little to do with intelligence. Just because someone was potty trained when he was still in his mother's womb does not mean he is smarter than the child who was potty trained at three and a half years of age.

This grouping and selection process does become an issue in terms of education because of how they are taught once in their group. The highest group (mostly girls and a few more developmentally advanced boys) gets to read more complex stories, learns more complex words, and gets asked more complex questions by the teacher. In the highest group, the teacher might ask questions such as:

- What do you think the main character was thinking?
- What would you have done if you were in that situation?
- What do you think will happen next?

These are all good thinking questions. But in the lowest and slowest group, the teacher might ask:

- What color shirt was the main character wearing?
- What was the dog's name?
- What did the main character do after that?

All are simple recall questions usually asked because the kids do not read very well. And why don't they read very well? They are boys and mature developmentally later than girls do. This becomes a huge issue because what starts out as a small gap in first grade grows larger every single year in school because you can't learn what you haven't been taught.

By the time the boys are actually developmentally ready to learn to read, they hate reading because they have been asked to do something they literally cannot do for years. Now that they are developmentally ready, they don't want to. Once a child has been placed in a low group, the chances of moving up are virtually nonexistent because he is now years behind in thinking, questions, and experiences. This process grows worse as the children go into middle and high schools because the top, most qualified teachers usually teach the top students. So, the students who need the best, most qualified teachers usually get the most inexperienced, novice teachers.

For beginning teachers, it has become a rite of passage to survive the first few years by teaching the low-track classes. For the students, it has become a self-fulfilling prophecy where they don't believe they can succeed, so they don't. The old movie *To Sir, With Love* is not a fiction story. It happens every year in virtually every middle and high school across the country.

These are the students who, for the most part, end up in the vocational education classes where they learn by doing. It isn't because it makes some sort of educational sense. It is because they have been so unsuccessful learning in the more abstract classroom environment. It isn't about intelligence. They just were punished because they developed later than their peers did.

In fact, if you really deeply consider developmental issues as an important factor in teaching and learning, you might conclude that the teaching and learning model from vocational education might need to be incorporated with all the other content areas. Perhaps what many students need is both the concrete (the application) and the abstract (the theory) both at the same time. It could provide students tools for life, assessment that is both embedded and obvious, clear and powerful goals and visions, and opportunities for celebrations of learning for students, parents, and the communities in which they live.

# Chapter 14

# The Purpose of Foreign Language

The study of foreign language is not about verb tense, grammar issues, being called Jose or Monika, or even learning to sing "Fruelige Weinachten" and serenading the other classes in the school the week before Christmas break. It is also not about memorizing sentences like, "Could you please direct me to the nearest bathroom?" in another language and then not being able to understand the directions given to you.

The content area purpose of foreign languages is the expression of the human experience in different contexts. It has everything to do with audience and how to adapt your communication style for that setting.

The majority of public school students will not in fact travel overseas to the country of the language they are studying. To learn a foreign language based solely upon the chance you might someday travel to Mexico, Spain, Germany, France, or Japan has little real-world applicability.

What is applicable is learning how to modify your communication skills and strategies based upon the audience you are attempting to communicate with. This ability to code-switch means expressing your human experience to adults, other peer groups, bosses, teachers, and parents in ways that are most effective. Each new group has its own language, vocabulary, culture, and shared understandings that make it important to understand and realize if you wish to get along or fit in. The study of a foreign language just extends that code-switching to include very different new words and structures.

The process of learning a foreign language is ultimately one of the major diversity tools that exist because, in terms of thinking skills, being involved in the learning of a foreign language provides the foundation for a big same/ different thinking activity. By its very nature, learning to communicate in another language with different words, sentence structure, and tonality raises "human-ness" questions for the learner. Human-ness issues include topics such as:

- Why am I the way I am?
- What would I be like if I grew up somewhere else?
- What holidays would I celebrate? What is worth celebrating?
- What does culture mean, and what makes mine special?
- Are we just people living in different places, or are we just different people?

By studying people in different places, students are allowed the opportunity to study themselves and their own culture. They are allowed the opportunity to consider what is human and what is idiosyncratic to their time and place. It is a creative exercise that continually stretches their minds and imaginations by asking:

- What if I lived somewhere else?
- What would I think about art?
- What kind of music would I listen to?
- What kind of clothes would be cool and in style?
- What would my name be and mean?
- And what kind of food would I eat? Would I really eat snails, grubs, or pig's feet if I lived somewhere else?

Cultural questions emerge such as:

- What would my role be in another culture?
- What are the expectations for someone like me?
- How might I be the same or different?
- Would living somewhere else make my life easier or harder?
- What are the unwritten rules in different places? What unwritten rules am I following without even being aware of it?
- Why are they the way they are?
- Who are their heroes?

When foreign language is taught well, students begin to view diversity more as a luck-of-the-draw issue rather than a competition issue. It is not who's right or wrong or who's living in a better place or has a better culture. It is about how humans adapt to that time and place in human ways. The shifting of perspectives becomes a foundational skill.

Humans are born with the ability to learn over two thousand different languages and dialects and can learn any one of them as easily as they learned their native tongue. In fact, learning more than one language when young is a painless process for the child because it is just more words, and that's what they are learning on a daily basis anyway. Learning another language is easy before humans are ten years old and, in fact, can be learned without an accent.

Waiting to teach a foreign language until middle school or high school is one of the clearest signs of a lack of developmental consideration for learning that exists in school today, along with teaching formal reading to boys in first grade and a lack of physical education on a daily basis for all students.

Learning more than one language provides students with more options and choices for communicating. They have access to new words and new tenses, new syntax and new tonality, and new and different body language. Foreign language can help students learn there are many ways versus only their way for everything that makes us human, and that's an important lesson.

## Chapter 15

# All Together

## *The Content Area Purposes*

Imagine for a moment that schools were oriented toward the content area purposes previously identified. This focus would begin in kindergarten and extend all the way through high school, every class and every day.

Every course would be aligned and provide tools and options to help our students live their lives as effectively as they could. Our students would have had the opportunity to learn and practice skills such as:

- Understanding themselves and others and the interactions between humans
- The ability to express their experiences with all sorts of words, through art and with music
- A method for noticing and solving problems on their own
- Processes to help them make good decisions
- The ability to recognize and describe patterns and look for and predict fundamental solutions

If these skills were taught and learned through concrete experiences, students would view learning as an ongoing lifelong venture and perhaps even as a creative experience. Our students would emerge from our schools as RE-people, people comfortable with change and able to add new experiences to old for deeper understanding. They would be reflective and review daily experiences and be able to reorganize, reconceptualize, and reframe their thoughts and patterns with new information and experiences. Relearning would be the daily norm.

Students would have access to many tools and options from which choices could be made. (If you only have a hammer, pretty soon, everything starts to look like a nail.) And knowing that choices exist gives one power. The power would lie in their hands, and they would have grown into the appropriate use of power through choices and decisions they have had and experienced through consequences. They might even still trust adults as partners in learning.

In life outside of schools, the complex real-world problems combine all the content area purposes. Different situations require a different priority of these content area purposes, but, ultimately, everything is connected. When this type of thinking is recognized and valued in a classroom, the teacher and the students approach learning as a system where they realize you must see both the forest and the trees at the same time. Individual skills are taught and seen as important as a function of the whole (the context).

In this type of setting, it becomes possible to meet both higher standards and deeper understanding for all our students. If we organize teaching and learning experiences with these content area purposes in mind, we would then be able to answer "Why do I have to learn this stuff?" in clear, powerful, and meaningful ways, as well as ask the following types of questions:

- Under what conditions do these traits emerge?
- What are the building blocks and sequences necessary to develop these skills?
- How do we structure the learning experiences?
- How do we tie this type of learning to the curriculum we already have?

*Section 3*

# Making Purpose Come Alive

*Chapter 16*

# Knowledge Needed

To review then, the content area purposes are as follows:

**Table 16.1   Content Area Purposes**

| Content Area | Purpose |
| --- | --- |
| Social Studies | The human experience |
| Language Arts | Expression of the human experience with words |
| Science | Problem-noticing and problem-solving |
| Mathematics | Patterns into symbols |
| Foreign Language | Expression of the human experience in different contexts |
| Physical Education and Health | Decision-making |
| Art | Expression of the human experience through two- and three-dimensional representations |
| Music | Expression of the human experience through sounds |
| Vocational Education | Life skills |

These content area purposes serve as the primary lens for learning each content area. From these content area purposes come visions (Senge 1990), which are measurable and worthy of celebrations. In the spiraling curriculum, the content area purpose is the center, the core, about which the curriculum spirals. The actual content area purpose words must be used on a daily basis by both the teacher and the students. And if and when there is no strong connection between what is to be taught and the purpose, then perhaps the content should be taught in a different way so it is aligned with the purpose(s).

The ability to use the content area purpose effectively and give the students good reasons for learning the material is a complex skill. It requires a deep understanding and is therefore knowledge-dependent (defined as "know, understand, and act upon"). Generally speaking, the shallowest type of knowledge can be referred to as surface-level understanding (Senge 1990), a definition level where the person knows the word and how to define it. This type of knowledge frequently results from a fact-based curriculum that strives to cover as much material as possible in as short a time as possible, ergo a mile wide and an inch deep.

Intellectual or theoretical understanding refers to definitions plus examples. Each item can be explained in depth, but only in isolation. This is the ability to identify all the parts of a cell, explain the structure and function of each part in isolation, and not see how one is related to the other.

Dynamic or felt understanding means the learner has seen the connection between the pieces, the felt or "aha" experience. He knows the parts, the definitions, the structure, and function. More importantly, he sees how the pieces work together. Words that usually indicate this type of understanding are "insight" or "interrelationships." This felt understanding is long-term and powerful. Patterns become evident, and modifications are realized. It is the lightbulb going off above the learner's head.

This deepest level of understanding is especially hard to achieve when the learner has not had multiple experiences. One person's felt meaning, even when shared, rarely translates into someone else's felt meaning. It is ultimately an individual experience. This type of understanding is so important, however, that any time dedicated to allowing it to happen is time well spent.

The key to the spiraling curriculum is that the purpose remains the same while more and more skills and strategies are learned. This allows more and more opportunities for all the students to get it. All new learning is tied to previous learning. All connections are emphasized on a daily basis. In reality, there is very little totally new learning going on. It is mostly an adaptation of something that has been learned before. It's all connected and hopefully to the purpose.

In order to make this type of learning come alive for the students, teachers must see both the forest and the trees of learning. They must deeply understand the individual skills (the trees) while, at the same time, realizing each skill exists only as a function within the whole (the forest). It is impossible to speak about one isolated tree in the forest without talking about the forest itself. Remember, it is all connected. For effective instruction, the trees and the forest might look something like the following:

Knowledge of Content + Knowledge about Our Students + Knowledge about How Learning Takes Place Tied to Vision and Aligned with Purpose

## KNOWLEDGE OF CONTENT

A depth of understanding about content does not mean only knowing more facts than your students do. It does also not mean staying one chapter ahead or focusing only on vocabulary words, definitions, and spelling. It certainly is not about using only one source of information for any kind of learning. It is about understanding content deeply, seeing and knowing the connections and big patterns that exist within each content area and topic.

It is knowing where the facts that are in the textbooks actually came from and the process by which they came into being. It is knowing and understanding content so well and so deeply that student learning mirrors the way that the experts in the field learn. Historians don't memorize history texts, scientists don't memorize vocabulary lists, writers don't write just for teachers, and mathematicians don't sit around and solve problems in a math book. Experts create and so should students.

Content knowledge must be understood so deeply that it becomes connected to everyday lives, every day and in every way. Content must be understood so deeply that every task is seen as a progression from simple to complex and connected to what is already known and what needs to be learned next.

The spiraling curriculum does not exist only for students, but also for the lifelong learners who are the teachers. Writing teachers need to write, science teachers need to do science, history teachers need to do history, physical education teachers need to do physical activities, and on and on. Teachers need to be the role models for the content they are teaching.

This model already exists in some content areas within schools. Typically, music teachers play music, art teachers make art, coaches are often old athletes, and most vocational teachers have emerged from their respective fields of welding, mechanics, sewing, building, and so forth.

It is only within the core content areas that having a theoretical level of understanding is deemed sufficient, and that is a shame because then that becomes the way they teach. Being able to do something fundamentally changes how you teach it.

Many extracurricular activities actually provide better models of content knowledge acquisition than traditional courses. School newspapers, yearbooks, plays and musicals, drama and speech contests, Model United Nations, and Junior Achievement are just a few examples of opportunities where students have the opportunity to learn content with a deep level of understanding.

The ability to do your content area requires an understanding beyond facts and memorization alone. It is literally being able to see both the forest and the trees. Skills are not just skills to be learned. Skills allow the participant to do the task better or more effectively than they were done before the skill was learned. They have a context.

You hammer and saw not just to hammer and saw, but to build something. That building is the context for the learning. You learn to count and play notes so you can make music, and you learn to shade and draw perspective so your picture will communicate what you want to communicate. You do not diagram sentences just to diagram sentences because, when you do, it has no context! You must connect it (give it context), or you will be hammering for hammering's sake.

Content issues are addressed in schools through curriculum, and curriculum needs to be rewritten so the context is clear, powerful, and evident to everyone: parents, students, and teachers. The context needs to be clearly identified so it sets the stage for the learning of individual and specific skills. A depth of understanding takes precedence over coverage. With a powerful context, content knowledge becomes embedded within the learning rather then the end result of learning.

## KNOWLEDGE ABOUT OUR STUDENTS

A depth of knowledge about content is no less or more important than the knowledge the teacher has about the students he is working with. Both types of knowledge are crucial and fundamentally intertwined in effective teaching. It is not enough to generalize to the first-grade class or freshman-level English or even AP chemistry. The teacher must know much more.

The teacher must be aware of gender issues, developmental issues, cultures, experiences the students bring to class, learning styles and types of intelligences they utilize, what students find funny and what they find tragic, problems they are experiencing and changes they are going through, music they listen to, and games they are playing on an individual level. Are they beginning to date or just playing with the idea of relationships?

To be an effective teacher requires a depth of understanding about the students he is working with: physically, emotionally, socially, intellectually, and morally. This type and depth of knowledge must exist if the teacher is to pick the right content at the right time for the students he is responsible for.

The teacher must have general student knowledge and then go beyond to knowledge of students as individuals. General categories of knowledge about our students include topics such as developmental windows, learning styles and types of intelligences, maturity levels, types of humor, learning strengths and weaknesses, brain processing skills and abilities, and attention spans. In public schools, the most important general knowledge topic is that of development, another name for change.

As students go through schools, they are constantly changing in body, in mind and thoughts, and in their relationships to and with others. The teacher must know who he is working with, if he hopes to do it effectively. This knowledge cannot be left to chance if the teacher is to make good decisions about the content he will utilize to help the students learn something important.

A continuum view of these topics may be useful in that, as its foundation, development is fluid with little or no absolutes. Students are where they are and do not necessarily fit into neat and tidy compartments or categories. They change from day to day and on the specific task at hand. Some continuums might be (and remember there are exceptions to every generalization):

## PROCESSING ABILITY

Totally Concrete ——————————————————————— Totally Abstract
This includes the use of hands-on materials and manipulatives, the level of understanding everyone is striving for, the transition between totally concrete to totally abstract, and the ability to represent things, thoughts, and ideas.

## WAITING ABILITY

Today Orientation ——————————————————— Future Orientation
This deals with relevance and the ability to put off something until sometime in the future. Speaking to fourth graders about when they are married clearly does not take this thinking process into consideration. Time frames for the future and the ability to make changes with that perspective in mind are clearly dependent upon the age and maturity of the students.

## MATURITY

Dependent ——————— Independent ——————— Interdependent
From parents and peers wanting to make decisions for themselves to understanding that each individual decision impacts everyone around him is important to understand about our students. A classic example is with middle school students who need parents to be at the mall, but don't want anyone

to know their parents are there. They are transitioning from dependence to independence, but need some help along the way.


## SOCIAL CONTEXT

Self —————————————— Group —————————————— Humanity
Another way of looking at this continuum is by watching how and with whom children play. The ability to interact with others and make decisions with others in mind changes as people mature and have different experiences. Some students are also geared more to social interactions while others develop later. To study the world and other cultures before they are developmentally ready wastes time.

Other continuums might include:

* Small motor skill development, which has major effects on the ability to read and write
* Physical development and changes such as losing teeth
* Puberty and growth spurts
* Humor from knock-knock jokes to physical humor to patterns with unexpected twists emphasizing the human condition

All are critical to understanding the students the teacher is working with on a daily basis. A moral continuum also plays a role as students develop their ideas about right and wrong, fair and equal, and justice, rights, and power.

The inability to take the knowledge of students into consideration results in frustration for both the teacher and the learners. For example, many time-on-task issues are related to the teacher's awareness of the activity-ness issues of development. When students have the ants-in-the-pants syndrome, is it because they are bad and naughty and need to be punished, or is it a lack of teacher consideration for the age and development of the students?

These general knowledge topics are important because they also help the teacher to understand the issue of normality for the students he is working with. He needs to have such a deep understanding that he realizes what normal is and the range of behaviors that fall into that category and understands when behaviors are so far out of the norm that they need to be addressed as soon as possible. Intuition is helpful, but a depth of knowledge and understanding is more useful when working with students, parents, and other adults who care about the student.

These topics provide a skeleton of topics and knowledge that must then be supplemented with specific knowledge about each individual within the group. It is also important to understand the individual experiences each student has to draw upon, such as family and cultural backgrounds.

One of the first years I taught, I had a young man who used poor language on a daily basis. I punished him regularly, sent him to the office, and kept him after school. I basically tried everything I knew how to do. Finally, I set up a parent conference because I wanted to talk to his parents very badly because their child used such bad and naughty language. I was chomping at the bit to fix that parent. I'd had nothing but problems, and no solutions seemed to work in respect to changing his language. I was ready to let them have it.

When the parent did come in for the conference, I found him to be coarse but supportive. He wanted to know what the little @x$%% had done now and what the %$##@ I wanted him to do to make it right. He was willing to beat the $**&^ out of the kid when he got home if that's what I wanted. Pretty much every single sentence had at least one swear word in it. The fog began to lift from my eyes.

At that exact moment, I realized the child was doing pretty darn good and what I had seen as a major issue was, in reality, rather immaterial. By the end of the conference, I was virtually begging the parent to let me handle it at school. "No, in reality, he's a joy to have in my class."

I gained perspective on the child as an individual and where he was starting from. That perspective does not give permission to lower the standards. Knowledge about individuals just tells you where to begin!

Teachers need to be aware of:

- The interests that students have, such as hobbies, crafts, and sports they like to participate in
- What they do with their free time
- Who their friends are
- Who their heroes are
- What other adults play a role in their lives besides their parents
- What TV shows they watch
- What movies interest them
- What books they like to read
- What computer games they play every single waking moment of their lives (if they could)

It is also important to know:

- What genetic dispositions they have related to learning such as learning styles and multiple intelligence propensities
- How they think and learn

- What strengths they bring to the class
- What weaknesses they need to overcome
- What problems they are experiencing
- What strategies they are using to solve them

This information is not a right or wrong issue that the teacher has to approve or disapprove. It is a "just is" issue. Without this type of information about the students in our schools, the search for relevance is like the search for the Holy Grail, long, drawn-out, and based on luck.

Relevancy may be defined as the following, what you are asking each student to learn right now is aligned with his individual needs today. Relevance is the intertwining of content knowledge with knowledge about our students. Content is selected with the future in mind, but teaches skills that are needed today. It aligns individual goals and ambitions with the content to be mastered.

Teachers who teach with relevance in mind exhibit a sense of "with-it-ness" with their students. They have the ability to move the students along the learning continuums with a sense of differentiated instruction (Tomlinson 2001) within the curriculum that accommodates individual strengths and interests.

Teachable moments are both designed into the learning activities and taken advantage of when they emerge spontaneously. Teaching for relevance takes advantage of the natural learning process versus learning because someone told you that you had to. Teaching with relevance in mind changes the classroom experience.

The ability to blend content knowledge with knowledge about our students sometimes results in redoing units of instruction so they are more coherently aligned. For example:

Let's say you teach in Montana, and the year is 2002. You teach fifth-grade social studies. Because you like history and because it is the bicentennial of Lewis and Clark, you have chosen to focus on them for the next unit of study. This content selection may be problematic. You have failed to take into account who your students are and the background they bring to the classroom. You must realize and act upon the fact that one-half of the students are Native American, and almost every single one of them has at least one relative living on one of the four major reservations surrounding your school. Celebrating Lewis and Clark, who "discovered" Montana, might be viewed with a slightly different perspective.

The teacher must look deeper into his understanding of content and his students if he wishes to pick a topic that really works for all students to learn. Perhaps, after further thought, he redefines his choice of topic as "explorers" and gives the students choices of explorers they wish to study: white explorers, black explorers, Native Americans explorers, male explorers, female explorers, boy explorers, and girl explorers, as large a selection of choices as possible.

The teacher needs to know that providing these choices will allow the students the opportunity to find some commonalities among people stepping into the unknown. You know this will intrigue them because they have already begun talking about the move to the middle school and sixth grade next year. In fact, you hope to have them understand that we are all explorers and this knowledge will help them be more confident in the big change next year and in the years to come.

Learning is fundamentally an individual activity that takes place within a group setting in schools. The ability to connect what students already know and understand to the topic at hand and then to align that knowledge with the vision and purpose requires an artist's touch. It also points to the importance of small class sizes where teachers have the time to learn about their students.

Looping and multi-age classrooms are both strategies that take this view seriously. Schools within a school attempt to do the same. Ultimately, what the teacher knows about his students must be the number-one criteria for selecting content topics and skills to be learned. This knowledge about his learners allows the teacher to clearly identify where the students are when the journey is begun. He can then make learning decisions on how to help them achieve the vision with the purpose in mind.

## LEARNING PROCESS KNOWLEDGE

In order to utilize content knowledge and knowledge about our students to achieve learning visions, you must also have a clearly defined process for how you believe people learn. You must also differentiate between memorization and learning. I would suggest looking at a model of learning from outside the school setting because people learn without lectures and tests on a daily basis.

For example, what have you learned recently? List five to ten things you have learned recently and then look at the words you have used to describe them. Frequently, people might say, "I learned how to cook, play a game, sew a quilt, do a PowerPoint presentation, and so forth." If you haven't learned anything new lately (shame on you), ask your own kids or kids in school. Almost always, learning something outside the school setting involves action.

Then ask yourself or others, how did you go about learning it? What were the steps in the process? Who helped, and when and what was their role? How did you know you had learned it well? How long did it take? How well did you do it the first, second, or third time? How many times did you fail before you mastered it? Have you mastered it? Why did you bother to learn it at all? Why is it worth your time and effort?

You must have a clear picture in your mind about how people learn because, without one, you cannot possibly structure a learning event for your students with any degree of success or confidence, beyond the luck factor.

Let us take a look at two scenarios as examples:


## SCENARIO 1


You have just moved to a new location and are in the process of meeting new people and getting acquainted with the area. You go to some parties, see some sites, and try some new restaurants. You meet someone new, and he asks if you know how to fish, ski, or camp. To which, you reply "No, but I would like to give it a try." Let us say for the sake of simplicity that the topic to be learned is ice-skating. While you have never had a pair of skates on, you have seen it on TV. So you make a date, and he picks you up. You get to the rink and are told to put on your skates. Even though you have never skated, you can put on your own shoes. The skates have laces like your hiking boots, so you put on your skates.

As you stand up, you wobble and grab the person who brought you. You begin to think that this might not be a simple as you had thought. You stagger to the ice and listen as your new friend offers words of encouragement. You look over the rink and see people of all ages whipping around the rink: old people, young people, and the incredibly young. All are making ice-skating look pretty simple. Your confidence rises, and you once more begin to think you will be able to skate.

You open the door and take your first step. Whoa! You almost fall. You are now holding on to your friend with a death grip. You are sure you have cut off all circulation in his arm. He tells you to relax and take some walking steps first. So while hanging on to him and the wall, you begin to take some baby steps. It isn't anything like what you have seen on TV, but at least you're not falling down yet. You stop now and then and give your friend a smile. You are going to live!

After a once-around the rink while hanging on to the wall, your confidence begins to grow, and you are ready for the next step, gliding. Your first attempts are all of four inches long, but at least it's not walking anymore. You continue with your mix of walking steps and gliding steps and have managed not to fall so far. Your friend now leaves you for a little skating on his own, and he makes it look so simple. You are bound and determined to skate like that someday. One more time around, you think you are ready to leave the wall. Your friend is back, and you take his arm.

Out you go. You are skating at kind of a rudimentary pace, but you are skating. You let go of your friend and take a big push. Wham! Down you go. Boy, is ice hard. You are sure you have broken your butt bone. If not broken, then you will have the world's biggest bruise tomorrow. Your friend is trying not to laugh, but the tears running down his cheeks gives him away. You smile grimly and attempt to get up. You are sure everyone in the arena is staring at you, but you strengthen your resolve, crawl onto your hands and knees, and, using your friend like a tree, crawl back onto your skates. More little steps and baby glides.

By the end of the evening, you are skating and have even managed to glide more than four inches at a time. You realize that, if you are going to skate well, it is going to take some practice and maybe even a lesson or ten. But it was fun, and you could see the possibility of success. Yes, you fell more than once, but it was fun. You and your friend also went out for a snack afterwards, and you seemed to connect, both talking about skating. He related his own learning experiences and crashes as well. You feel connected. The rink is open this Saturday afternoon as well.

## SCENARIO 2

You enroll in a class, Ice Skating I. You walk in, sit down in a desk, and wait for the teacher to come in. When he does, he first hands out a syllabus and then a book and then begins talking about the mechanics of skating. He assigns the first chapter in the *Ice-Skating for Dummies* book and sends you home. You read the first chapter, which talks about the parts of an ice skate and how the ice rink works. You even do the questions at the end of the chapter that asks about the parts of the ice skate and how the ice rink works.

You attend the next class where there is a quiz about the parts of the ice skate and how an ice rink works. Then the teacher lectures, using a Power-Point presentation, about the parts of the ice skate and how the rink works. He spends forty-five minutes talking about the curve in the blade and how it works and how real skaters have different kinds of curves for different kinds of skating. He then assigns chapter 2, "The Mechanics of Skating."

This continues for eight weeks with quizzes, tests, more lectures, and PowerPoint presentations. After passing the final exam, which you pass with a 96 percent, you have completed the course with an A. You are now ready for Ice Skating II.

Which scenario truly represents human learning, and which is artificial? This is a huge point. In fact, this example may be the key point to the entire conversation.

Fact-based learning deals with memorization and learning about something. It does not focus on actually doing what is to be learned. For example, when taking a course in literature, does one actually write literature, or does one read someone else's works and then memorize the teacher's interpretation? In *The Old Man and the Sea*, which I had to read in high school, does the shark really represent evil, or is it just a big fish, which happened to be in the right place at the right time?

The real learning in textbook recitation is learning how to remember what the teacher thinks is important just long enough to pass the test and then to forget and repeat the process. Many people find this process to not be worthwhile.

Learning as it exists outside the school setting (a generalization) usually involves doing something. In fact, when someone says he learned something, it usually means he can now do something he could not do before. For example, I learned how to play hacky-sack, cook a pheasant, ice-skate, use a computer, and so forth. The interesting thing about learning for oneself is that, when done well and with depth, facts are learned and remembered within the process. They do not stand alone. They have context! Learning is not content-free.

If we could model classroom learning on the learning model that people utilize outside the school setting, we might discover that certain components exist.

*Chapter 17*

# The Role of . . .

## THE ROLE OF PERSONAL VISION

One of the major differences between school learning and learning outside the school setting is that, when people learn things for themselves, the point of the learning is clear. People know what they want to learn. They see where they want to go, what they want to do or learn, and what they want to accomplish. They also choose what they are going to learn and accept the fact that learning something now will mean some sort of change in behavior. In fact, this is a fundamental learning point. The vision for learning has to be strong enough to change current behaviors or no real learning will take place.

It could be said that all learning is egocentric. You learn what you want to learn when you want to learn it because you think it is useful or beneficial in some sort of way. Therefore, when you are motivated to learn, it means you want to learn something because it is important to you and you alone.

The reasons for learning are numerous, but they ultimately boil down to you want to because it meets your needs at that time and place. I want to learn how to ice-skate, ski, teach, and so forth for my own good reasons and because I want to. It is important enough right then to cause me to change my behaviors or thought processes. If the learning continues and is deep, then the learning goes way beyond winning or losing. It becomes a self-actualization issue (Maslow 1999).

In learning outside the school setting, expertise is also obvious. There are clear differences between levels of mastery. How a novice does the task is clearly different than how an expert does the same exact task. This helps the learner in that, if he wishes to achieve mastery, the vision pulls the learner forward to continue learning and achieving the vision.

Competition may be a part of the activity, but, in reality, the greatest competition is internal, even when playing against others. Sorting for levels of achievement or quality is based on criteria that are clear and most generally agreed upon, but, as in everything, the interpretation is still subjective, especially at the highest levels of performance. There are large gaps between a novice and someone who is competent as well as someone who is competent and an expert, but there are fine lines between the experts themselves.

Because learning outside the school setting is usually a choice by the learner, it has some relevance or meaningfulness to the individual. It's his vision. This relevance makes the learning journey, the acquisition of new patterns of behavior, thoughts, or ideas worthwhile to the learner. This relevance is crucial in that all deep learning involves risk. Risk is a part of all learning and is a part of what makes the learning fun. Unfortunately, the term "fun" has a poor educational connotation, so let us give it a learning definition.

My family travels quite a bit by car, and we frequently travel up to twenty-four hours in one shot. Sometimes, we stop at a rest area to get out for some exercise and frequently play the game of tag. Now we range in age from forty-nine to eight. To be fun for everyone requires some special rules. Usually when playing tag, it is not fun to be it all the time.

It is also not fun to never be it at all. There seems to be an individual ratio of it to not it that determines if the game is fun or not for the individual. Some people like to be it quite a bit while others are happy to almost never be it at all. The individual risk ratio between success and failure is what makes the game fun.

We may therefore educationally define fun as appropriately challenging. The risk involved in learning must be a delicate balance between the right number of successes to the acceptable number of failures along the way, if the learner is to accept the challenge. Learning involves change; change is a high-risk activity. Relevance makes risk manageable. Learning must be structured in such a way that the balance between successes and failures falls within individual boundaries if the learner is to see the experience as fun.

Too hard means the risk of achieving success is too great, and the chances for success are too slim. Too easy means the game is boring. There is virtually no risk of failure at all. At either end of the continuum, learning is not viewed as fun. If there is no fun, learning occurs at the surface level at best. Remember, educationally speaking, fun means acceptable risk, not no risk at all. When left to their own devices, people will not continuously make choices that bore them because being bored is not fun.

The spiraling curriculum comes into play in that it always provides the next vision for learning, the next risk to be undertaken. This may involve changing the rules in such a way to modify the risks or may involve adding another skill or layer of complexity to the task to keep the learning fun. Doing more of the same does not constitute more fun whereas changing something may.

Many years ago, when kids played sandlot games, this idea was basic understanding. When the neighborhood kids got together to play baseball, there were never exactly eighteen players, and they were never of the same ability level. Therefore, to keep people from taking their ball and going home, kids learned to modify the rules to keep the game fun and interesting. Pitcher's hand (when you didn't have a first baseman), ghost runners, right field was out, certain players had to hit left-handed, and so forth were developed to keep the game fun. It wasn't fun to get beat one hundred to nothing, and it wasn't fun to never get a hit, so rules were modified, and new skills were developed. Fun kept people coming back and playing more.

At its core, the spiraling curriculum must have an enduring point or purpose that all learning revolves about. The purpose must be enduring and complex enough so learning may continue beyond any single skill. The purpose drives the spiraling curriculum, it provides the continuous strand for all learning within the curriculum area, and it may be viewed as the Velcro that holds it all together.

In sports and music in particular, the spiraling curriculum makes so much sense that it is embedded within the experiences. A beginning basketball player learns how to dribble a ball, and this skill continues to be taught and practiced throughout the player's career. In music, the scales are taught to beginning musicians and practiced from then on. Levels of expertise become a part of the continued visioning process.

The same skills are taught, practiced, and modified to different levels of performance. All golfers can hit a drive, but the quality of each drive varies significantly depending upon the skill of the individual, just as all pianists can play notes and count, but the quality varies from individual to individual. In reality, there are very few major patterns of behavior within any content field, but there are an infinite number of variations of each theme. Having a comprehensive core or purpose allows connections and modifications to be made by the learner and to scaffold new learning off previous learning.

Therefore, the spiraling curriculum may be considered a skills-based approach tied to a solid learning structure. It can be structured to be developmentally appropriate for any learner and can provide a lifelong learning model in that there is always something new to learn and practice.

A well-designed spiraled curriculum allows the learner the opportunity to travel the learning journey from "unconsciously unskilled" (you don't know what you can't do) to "consciously unskilled" (you are now aware of what you can't do) to "consciously skilled" (you put the new pattern into practice) to "unconsciously skilled" (the new pattern is now a part of who you are).

Ignorance is truly bliss because you are not even aware of all the things you do not know and cannot do.

The vision sets the journey because a point in every direction is the same as no point at all. The vision drives the learner to begin and sustain his journey and find the changes within to be worthwhile. Without such a vision, all you have is good ideas.

## THE ROLE OF THE LEARNING JOURNEY

Once you have a vision and you view it as a real vision for yourself, which means it is strong enough to change your behaviors and thought patterns, the journey is begun. You have chosen to undertake this journey for what you consider to be good reasons. It meets your needs, and you want to. You are ready to learn because it is relevant to you, and you are driven by the vision. You know you need to know something specific, learn new skills, and practice and relearn patterns of behavior. And you are ready. The path is set before you with steps, goals, and objectives as markers along the journey to your vision.

You also realize that the learning process will never be totally finished. Beyond the vision lie more visions, but they will have to wait until this current journey is completed. You have learned other things before, and you understand the journey will be long and difficult. There will be moments filled with doubts and frustrations when you may wish to quit, but there will also be moments filled with joys, highs, and celebrations.

Emotion is always part of the learning journey. You realize the learning will occur in fits and starts. It is not a smooth line of growth, but one with peaks and valleys. It says, "You need more practice before you can move on." It says, "It's time to get it on right now!" You also know you may need some help along the way, but you have a support group and some mentors waiting in the wings. You are ready.

You realize that, even though you have support, learning is a solitary, individual experience. Learning has to be earned by each individual. It cannot be given to anyone. You will have to discover knowledge for yourself, make connections for yourself, learn new skills for yourself, and practice those skills by yourself until they are part of who you are. It is your vision and therefore your journey, and no one can take it for you or save you from it.

Your learning journey will be governed by the experiences you have along the way. As your experiences grow, the need for new patterns becomes evident, and you recognize the need for new rules and patterns. These experiences encourage or, in fact, demand growth and are opportunities for more and deeper learning. Both failure and success are part of the process, and you come to realize that you learn from both.

These experiences push you beyond your comfort zone, but you soon realize it's not such a scary place to be. In fact, you become addicted to higher risk and learning, especially the feeling when you get it, when the pieces fall into place and you see the new pattern as clearly as you see the nose on your face. "Aha! I get it. Why didn't I see it before, and why didn't other people tell me?" you say to yourself. But then you realize that they couldn't because it's your journey. They wouldn't want to deprive you of the emotion, even if they could.

You begin to experiment, which means to not know the outcome, more and more, keeping the vision in sight. You play and play with your experiences, thoughts, and ideas until you begin to figure it out on your own. Failure is part of experimenting and playing. Pretty soon, you realize that failures actually help you figure out what you have left to learn. They clarify where you are on your learning journey! You become comfortable not doing it perfectly the first time. It's not your expectation. If and when you do it perfectly the first time, you figure you didn't set your goals high enough.

You practice your new skills and practice them. You try them and then practice them some more, but you don't mind because they are crucial to the vision you have. Sometimes, you wish you could learn them faster or easier, but that's just not the way it is.

So you practice some more. You give more time and more effort because it's important to you. Sometimes, you need to find out exactly where you stand in terms of your journey, so assessments or performances sometimes come in handy. They help clarify where you are and what you have left to learn. Each individual skill that has been learned provides a checkpoint on the learning journey. They are especially useful when seen as individual pieces aligned with the vision.

Sometimes along the journey, you need some help. Questions emerge and need to be answered, but they are your questions, and you need the answers when you need the answers. You come to realize you need just enough information at that time and at that place so your journey can continue. You don't need or even want a ton of information about what it is. You want just enough information to keep you going because, when you need it, you need it badly.

Sometimes when you are on your journey, you encounter others who are also on their own personal journeys, sometimes similar to your own. Some are further along in their journeys while others have just begun. Some are younger; some are older. Some are smarter, and others are not as smart. Some are in a hurry; others just take their time. But they are all on the journey of learning.

You come to realize that learning is not so much driven by age as it is by the appropriateness of the learning journey itself. Learning has to do with vision, the journey, the skills, and expectations that have been set. It is a journey, not a race, and is determined by the individual learner for he is striving toward his vision.

But there are similarities among those on learning journeys, so you feel connected. You are all striving to learn something and to do something new and different for you. You realize that many of you have the need to share your learning experiences and the journey you are on. You wish to demonstrate the learning with an audience of people who truly care about you and your learning.

The sharing lends credence to your learning. Some learnings are worth being celebrated. Those experiences of visions being achieved are the emotional highs of a journey. The vision has been realized! It is a celebration not just for the individual, but also for everyone who has played any kind of role along the way. The celebration of learning connects people in ways that nothing else can. It sets the tone for the next vision, same purpose.

## THE ROLE OF SOCIAL SUPPORT

The hardest way to undertake a learning journey is to do it alone. It can be done, but facing the uncertainties alone and finding the right information at the right time always by yourself can be an overwhelming proposition. The learning journey is hard and long. For most people, it is best done with help, both emotional and informational.

Mentors play a pivotal role for the travelers on their learning journeys. They can be formal or informal, coaches, friends, parents, teachers, or other travelers or adults along the way. No matter who they are, they must understand the process of learning and role of support. They must know when to listen and speak and what the learner needs at that exact moment to be successful, not what he wants to give them.

Mentors must be able to provide emotional and unconditional support when the learner is tired, frustrated, already working at peak levels, discouraged, or stuck and especially when he wants to give up on his vision and quit. They must have the skills to provide encouragement, empathy, or a kick in the seat of the pants if that is what the learner needs, and they must be able to distinguish when each is required.

The best mentors must also be able to provide informational or skills-based support as well. Their own content knowledge must be deep and interconnected, and the pattern of learning must be explicit. They need to know what's right in terms of skills and patterns and provide information to refine the learning currently taking place. They need to be able to provide nonjudgmental approval for the abilities and skills of the learner as well as provide feedforward (future-oriented) information to make it better the next time.

Mentors must also be able to understand and recognize the changing roles they are required to play along the learning journey. At the beginning of a journey, they need to be able to provide basic skills and support, later less and less information, and finally friendship and camaraderie. The roles need to be based on levels of expertise, experiences, and where in the learning process the travelers are.

Perhaps the most important role of the mentor is to be the keeper of the vision. He must hold the vision in his hands as if it were a fragile, easily shattered vessel, which it is. The vision must be part of the daily language and serve as the number-one criteria for making daily choices. Each decision needs to be framed as either helping or hindering the achievement of the vision. The mentor must help the novice keep the vision burning brightly, or the vision will soon just be another idea whose time has not yet come.

Teams, cliques, groups, yearbook, newspapers, bands, and drama clubs are all examples of school activities where students share some vision and have chosen to participate in making that vision come to life. They are individuals within the whole where each personal vision is aligned with the shared vision of the group. They are on "a journey alone holding hands."

These types of activities frequently represent the best case for learning in schools settings. They each have a strong "we" focus where interdependence among the individuals is required. Each individual has an important, although different, role, and the success of all is dependent upon the cumulative success of the individuals. My success and your success are determined by our success is a basic functioning part of these types of groups.

## THE ROLE OF THE TEACHER

The most effective teacher integrates three types of knowledge:

1. He must have content knowledge that is deep enough so patterns and themes are clearly seen as applicable to the daily lives and times of his students.
2. He must also know his students well enough to know their individual strengths and weaknesses and tie new content to what they already know. He must know where each student is on the learning continuum.
3. He must understand the learning process so deeply that he can structure classroom learning experiences to mirror learning experiences that occur naturally outside the school setting.

Unfortunately, even a teacher who possesses these three types of knowledge may still not have enough knowledge to make the learning come alive or be relevant to the learners. He must also be able to align that knowledge with the visions of his students and the purpose of his content. Only when a teacher can combine all the knowledge he possesses and align it to visions and purpose can he put it together and sell it to the students so they want it!

## THE ROLE OF VISION

Using Peter Senge's (1990) explanations of current reality, vision, and purpose, a vision may be identified as something that is measurable and achievable. Some examples of visions might be running a five-minute mile, becoming a National Board Certified Teacher, or spending ten minutes per day alone with each of your children. The vision must be clear and obvious and of such personal worth that it is used as motivation to change patterns that already exist.

Vision achievement must be the criteria by which all daily decisions are made. They are not just good ideas. They are ideas worth fighting for, and the fight takes place on a daily basis. Once a vision has been established, only two options exist: work toward your vision or decide you like where you are at more than you want the vision. There are no other options once a vision has been established.

A purpose is much more general than a vision and, as such, is not really measurable. Some examples might be getting into shape, becoming the best teacher you can be, or having a close relationship with each of your children. Purposes are intrinsic, deep, and enduring and play a major role in that, once a vision has been established and met, the purpose remains to drive the next vision.

A schematic that Senge (1990) uses is visually very interesting and shows the relationship between the pieces:

Current Reality ——— Goals and Objectives ——— Vision ——— Purpose Your current reality is what exists today at this moment in time. It includes what you know, who you are, the experiences you can call upon, the relationships you have with others, and what is and is not important to you right now. You live in your current reality, and your current reality is a function of who you are and the experiences you have had. Therefore, your current reality also changes from day to day, if you choose to let it.

When you have a purpose (and you may have more than one) and you wish to act upon that purpose, you establish a vision as something you want more than you currently have. Usually, the vision is large and worthy of a great deal of effort.

To help you work toward your vision, goals and objectives are established as markers for the journey. Goals and objectives help you stay on track and provide small victories and celebrations to mark your progress. Each goal and objective that is met, of course, changes your current reality because, once a journey has been undertaken, the traveler is no longer the same. "You can never go home" is true because life's experiences fundamentally change a person who is on a journey.

The schematic is drawn as a straight line, and that may be its major shortcoming. Life happens, and therefore, most frequently, the line or the journey is more circuitous than was planned. Side trips occur or present themselves. Time estimates are off, and it is sometimes harder to learn something than was anticipated. The traveler must adapt to these circumstances while keeping the vision in mind on a daily basis.

Let's look at an example that might make this more concrete. For example, let's use building a home:

Imagine for a moment that you have decided you want a new home. That is your purpose, a home for you and your family. You analyze your current reality in terms of money available, type of environment, houses you have been in and liked, and houses you would never want to live in. You do more research clarifying exactly what you think you want. You finally narrow your choices down to building a house. You must now decide what type of house to build. When you finally decide and have the blueprints drawn up, you now have a vision.

You set goals and objectives and perhaps even formulate a timeline for the project. You contact the bank for a loan, find and buy the site, and contact the contractor, all with the end in mind, a home. As the project gets underway, delays happen, like bad weather, poor scheduling, and delays in materials arriving when promised. As the house is built, you continue to modify the plans, adding space here, changing materials there, extending deadlines, and getting more money, but the vision of building your house keeps you moving forward.

There are points during the project where you want to bag it all and quit. The frustrations seem insurmountable, and the delays are killing you. But you persevere, and things get better. Each major piece that is accomplished provides you with a minor victory. The foundation is being poured, the walls are up, the roof is completed, the drywall is hung, and the front door is installed. Rooms are painted, floors are laid, and the big day finally arrives. You are ready to move in.

You celebrate with a housewarming party, a celebration of epic proportions for your vision has been realized. The house is mostly done. You now realize that, while your vision has been realized, your purpose continues to drive you forward. You wanted a home, not just a house, so the journey continues.

Visions are crucially important in working toward your purpose(s) in life. They are what is worth achieving. They are concrete and measurable. Most importantly, they are worth celebrating for they signify achievement, hard work, and perseverance.

Visions must be strong enough to change current patterns of behavior. In other words, you must want the vision more than you want to keep doing what you are currently doing. When it's time for decisions, the vision must be the major criterion that is considered.

Many years ago, I used to smoke cigarettes on a fairly regular basis. I knew they were bad for me and they were not congruent with the rest of my relatively healthy lifestyle (my purpose), but I still smoked. When my wife and I decided to have children, I took that opportunity to also set a vision for myself, to quit smoking and realign my lifestyle with my purpose.

I also decided I needed a little help to spur me toward my vision. I decided to reward myself when I achieved the vision by buying myself a new leather motorcycle jacket at the end of my first year as a nonsmoker. I was heavily into motorcycling at the time and wanted that jacket very badly. With money being tight because I was a classroom teacher, it was something I probably would not have purchased otherwise. So I began my journey.

The situation was, however, compounded by the fact that, every other Wednesday night, I played pool with my father-in-law and six of his friends. This was problematic because, out of the eight pool players, six people smoked. I clearly remember standing in people's basements playing pool and having a running argument in my head:

- "How much do I want a smoke versus how much do I want that jacket?"
- "If I had a smoke tonight, I could start the year again tomorrow!"
- "Maybe if I just breathe really deep in this smoky air, I can have a smoke without really smoking!"

There were times when I almost gave in, and there were times when I questioned my vision, but I wanted to be healthy for my kids. I really wanted that jacket. In fact, I had already picked it out and even decided when and where to get it. It was real, and I wanted it badly!

Well, I made the year and bought the jacket. It only took about three more years to not really want a smoke. I still have that jacket, and I always will because, without that jacket (the vision), I might still be smoking today.

Visions are also not about winning or losing, and this is perhaps the most common error people make when setting visions for themselves or their teams. They set visions such as go undefeated, win the state title, or be conference champions. Those types of visions miss the point entirely. In fact, they are negative visions because they are based on fear of failure.

True visions ultimately deal with learning and doing. They concern the individual's or team's life's potential, way beyond merely winning and losing. They speak to playing well, to playing to your potential. If you do play to your potential, then you will increase the chances of victory. Visions deal with personal achievements where coming in last in a race is worth celebrating with joy and enthusiasm and a feeling of accomplishment is no less important than the winner of the race.

For those who make winning and losing the vision, does one loss really mean an entire season was a waste? How shallow is that? That type of thinking negates all the time, struggle, effort, joy, and anticipation that went into the learning and preparing for the vision.

When winning is the only measure for success, cheating becomes just another strategy to make it happen. When winning is the vision, competitors do not seek support from each other. They are taught to hate each other. There is no joy among the participants. In fact, even though the players love the same game, spend time doing the same thing, and maybe even have the same heroes, they view each other only as obstacles to their isolated visions. The vision has been distorted into a manipulation rather than a journey of learning and discovery.

The idea that vision must be aligned with purpose and deep, enduring concepts and values helps us set visions that are perhaps more noble than just winning and losing. Purpose exists even after a vision has been achieved. Purpose acts to set the next vision and the next learning journey. To have a home goes way beyond building a house. To stop smoking is just one part of a healthy lifestyle. As you undertake and achieve visions, you are changed. You have been re-created.

## THE ROLE OF SHARED VISIONS

In a classroom or on a team, the strongest vision is a shared vision that emerges from all the individual visions. Everyone must be able to see his own personal vision within the shared vision of the group. It must align everyone's individual vision and act to change current patterns of behavior that enhance the shared vision of the group in ways. It must also be aligned with the clear, deep, and meaningful purpose of the learning activity itself.

Without a shared vision and purpose for learning in the classroom, the textbook becomes the curriculum rather than a resource. Because it is not clear what is worth learning in many classrooms, every fact is given equal value.

Discipline problems exist for those students who do not know what they are striving toward because they do not buy in to the idea that facts are all there is. Relevance becomes based on hope. The teacher hopes the students will see the relevance of the material later in their lives.

Another problem of a shallow vision is that there is no way of self-correcting or self-monitoring in the system to tell you if you are getting there because you don't know where you have to go, other than finishing the book. Teachable moments are not designed into the lesson plans because the lesson plans are to cover certain material. In fact, the students get in the way! The vision becomes "to cover the content and finish the book," which results in learning typified by "an inch deep and a mile wide."

Passion for teaching within this fact-based model is translated into the interest you have in the subject and content you are teaching. Student enthusiasm and passion is a direct relationship to the amount of connection they feel with the teacher. Unfortunately, this becomes a trust issue between teacher and student.

When the teacher tells their students that the material is fun, interesting, and awe-inspiring and then the students do not find that to be true for them, trust is broken. The teacher's actions, enthusiasm, and words act like a promise. The students will find the material interesting and relevant. When they don't, the promise is broken.

In a classroom or on a team where the vision is shared and aligned with the purpose, things are much different. The passion for both teaching and learning emerges from the desire to reach the vision. Wanting the vision creates the energy for change and learning. It is part of the everyday experience where teacher and learners are on a journey together. It is part of the language and criteria used to make daily decisions and is where content comes into play.

These types of classrooms are both goal-oriented and skills-based. Skills must be learned if the goals are to be met. They do not sit isolated as important only for themselves. Teachable moments abound because everyone is on the journey. When they ask questions (and ask they will) about how things are done, how they are doing, what comes next, and where to find this or that, there exists at that specific moment in time a natural emotional tie-in between the learner and the learning. They are ready to learn and ready to remember for the long term.

Assessment is a natural part of this type of learning process because people want to know how they are doing in relationship to the skill and the goal and toward the vision. Not meeting expectations (failures) is viewed as part of the learning experience. While not something to look forward to, it helps everyone clarify the current reality, where you are in relationship to where you thought you were. Learning begins to have a future orientation in the now. What you are learning today is tied directly to what you need to learn tomorrow, if you are to reach your vision.

True shared visions are also not monopath. Because shared visions emerge from personal visions (personal relevance), there are naturally many paths to the same destination (vision). Telling this type of classroom teacher to include multiple intelligences or differentiate lessons is redundant because it happens naturally based on individual student needs and interests. Diversity of students is not a divisive issue because meeting everyone's needs through visions, goals, and skills is a fundamental structure of the classroom design. All learning is options-based toward the highest of standards, individual potential.

When the students and the teacher in these classrooms are all on a journey together (alone holding hands), support toward and for one another begins to emerge. Learning is not a competition, nor does it act as a sorting mechanism. Learning is what all people do, and everyone needs a little help along the way.

A sense of group identity begins to emerge. When this occurs, individual differences begin to enhance everyone's learning rather than get in the way. Some are good at writing, some are good at singing, some are good at computers, and some are good at running. When this type of classroom is done well, everyone is good at something. Not only are they good as individuals, they also use their talents for the betterment of the group itself. If you know something that will help me on my journey, please help me, and I will do the same for you.

This support can extend beyond the classroom walls as well. When the teacher is not the only expert in the classroom, pretty soon, everyone starts looking for experts anywhere he can find them, depending on what needs to be learned at that time. Parents, grandparents, friends, neighbors, mentors, community experts, construction workers, secretaries, doctors, and lawyers, the whole world is filled with experts once you start looking. Community connections become the norm, and the classroom walls are things to hang stuff on, not boundaries for learning.

In this type of classroom, there are also celebrations! Celebrations of the learning journey undertaken and visions met are to be shared with all those who have provided any type of support for the learners in the classroom, informational or emotional. Goals and objectives were met, skills were learned, achievements were noted, perseverance was recognized, obstacles and frustrations were laughed at, and hope was reignited. There is worthiness and appreciation for all the differences that helped everyone achieve the vision. It's a celebration of learning in the truest sense of the term! There is joy in learning.

# THE ROLE OF PURPOSE

If vision is where content and skills come into play, then what role does purpose fill? There must be a purpose. There must be some idea, some driving force that provides context for the visions. The purpose must be intrinsic, deep, enduring, applicable, and worthy of the learner's time, resources, and effort. It must be the language used every single day to help keep the vision alive.

The purpose must be the criteria by which all visions are selected. This means curriculum and content decisions, teaching and learning decisions, behavior decisions, rules and procedure decisions, and assessment decisions. The entire classroom environment must be aligned with the purpose(s).

Purpose emerges from thoughtful consideration of what is seen as the point of learning and what we wish for our children when they leave our schools. Purpose emerges when we thoughtfully and critically study what we are currently doing and compare it to our highest hopes for all our children. Clear and explicit purpose allows for connections and support between generations. Adults can reflect upon their life experiences and see that those ideas truly enhance the quality of an individual's life. Those ideas, purpose, are worth striving for and are seen as relevant to both student and adult.

As a cohesive group, the content area purposes point to individuals leaving their schooling experiences with the knowledge, skills, and dispositions to act as self-actualized citizens in a democratic society. They know and understand themselves, others with whom they interact, and the context for those thoughts, actions, and beliefs (the human experience). They communicate those experiences effectively through words, sounds, and representations while modifying those ideas in different contexts (language arts, music, art, and foreign language).

They notice and explain patterns that are both useful and predictive (mathematics). They notice and solve problems effectively and systematically (science) and learn from the decisions they have made (physical education/health). Last, they see the connection between ideas and actions (vocational education).

Students whose educational experiences are focused with these ends in mind are able and willing to be active participants in a democratic society because they see and understand their role within the larger context of life. They are on their journey toward self-actualization because their needs (safety, power, fun, freedom and love, and belonging) have been met developmentally throughout their schooling experiences. Schooling has served its purpose. Teachers have answered, "Why do I need to know this stuff?" in powerful, passionate, and relevant ways.

This book attempts to make the case that the content area purposes are the cumulative purpose for schooling today. The content area purposes need to be the core of the spiraling curriculum. They need to be used in such a way as to align content knowledge, student knowledge, and knowledge of the learning process with learning visions so relevance exists for the learners.

**Table 17.1   The Content Area Purposes**

| Content Area | Purpose |
|---|---|
| Social Studies | The human experience |
| Language Arts | Expression of the human experience with words |
| Science | Problem-noticing and problem-solving |
| Mathematics | Patterns into symbols |
| Foreign Language | Expression of the human experience in different contexts |
| Physical Education and Health | Decision making |
| Art | Expression of the human experience through two- and three-dimensional representations |
| Music | Expression of the human experience through sounds |
| Vocational Education | Life skills |
| Schooling | Self-actualized citizens in a democratic society |

## Chapter 18

# The Compelling Why

Providing answers to "Why do I have to know this stuff?" is a powerful activity. It means the teacher has explicitly examined and pondered his content, curriculum, and students. He is attempting to make those connections explicit for his students in an attempt to enhance the quality of their lives, today and in their future.

The Compelling Why is the teacher's first attempt to convince each and every student that what is to be learned is worthy of his time, resources, and effort. The teacher attempts to make the case that the learning they are asked to do will meet their individual needs, help them live their lives more productively today, and help them in the future as well. The teacher also recognizes that each student is different with his own set of unique strengths and weaknesses. Therefore, while the vision for learning is clear and powerful, the paths to achieve the vision are numerous.

Because everyone is working toward the same vision in his own way, helping each other learn and sharing individual strengths becomes the norm. Even the teacher is on the learning journey because each individual student is working toward the vision in his own unique way. In fact, classrooms where students are too similar actually hurts student learning. "We are in this together" really means what it says and includes the teacher as well as every individual student.

Course content and curriculum play an essential role as the platform for learning, not the end unto itself. Curriculum is viewed through the content area purpose lens in order to generate visions that meet student needs. Purpose drives the learning visions. Those visions drive content selection.

The Compelling Why also requires that the teacher be both artist and salesperson. He must have the ability to paint both the forest and the trees for his students and do it in such a way that the students want the painting and want it enough to change their current behaviors. This systems approach to learning ties the skills to be learned (goals and objectives) to the vision and purpose. The skills represent the trees while the vision and purpose represent the forest. At the deepest level of learning, you cannot talk about one without talking about the other. They are too interconnected.

The Compelling Why combines all the types of teacher knowledge with vision and purpose and attempts to communicate these relationships to both students and parents. Teacher passion emerges from the belief that the learning journey to be undertaken will fundamentally change student lives for the better and not necessarily easier for ignorance truly is bliss. The vision aligned with purpose creates the energy for learning and change. When the learning vision is achieved, it is truly worthy of celebration.

## GETTING STARTED: "THE COMPELLING WHY"

The Compelling Why is a daily task for the teacher that varies in length and content depending on where the learning task is within the unit of instruction. At the beginning of a unit of instruction, the Compelling Why might be twelve to fifteen minutes in length because the teacher is attempting to make the case for relevance for the entire unit of learning. After that, a daily Compelling Why might be only from two to five minutes in length, connecting what was learned yesterday to what is to be learned today and to what is to be learned tomorrow. Therefore, today's task is relevant not only unto itself, but also in relationship to yesterday and tomorrow (the vision).

## COMPELLING WHY STRUCTURE

1. Pick and tell a story from your student's lives that points to the need for the content area purpose.
2. Share how working toward the content area purpose will enhance their quality of life.
3. Share the learning vision that is aligned with the purpose.
4. Share the goals and objectives along the learning journey.

## STEP 1

Pick and tell a story from your student's lives that points to the need for the content area purpose. In order to point out the need for the purpose, the teacher must use content area purpose language on a regular basis. He must say the actual words every day and for every activity. Posting the content area purpose in the classroom is even better. The teacher must use the one content area purpose that is directly aligned to the specific content being emphasized by the unit of instruction or the specific learning activity.

If, for example, you were teaching a unit on simple machines (a science unit), then problem-noticing and problem-solving would be the content area purpose you would need to reference. You would need to say the actual words and refer to the content area purpose every day and for every learning activity.

Besides just using the words themselves, the teacher also needs to connect the need for the purpose to examples from the students' lives that prove to the students that the need for learning is genuine. (Today! Right Now!) The teacher must point to the need for the content area purpose using examples that are specific and real to the students at that point in time.

Stories from student lives must be used to make this point. The teacher heard a student say this or saw a student do that, or a student shared this experience with the teacher. The story describes one specific incident that explicitly points to the need to learn the content area purpose. Good stories put listeners into the experience with the use of details, thoughts, pauses, actions, and emotions. The story itself must be so specific that each student imagines the story being told is about him.

An excellent story format is that of an Aesop's fable, like the tortoise and the hare or the lion and the mouse. The story has a moral. In the case of the Compelling Why, the moral is the explicit need for the content area purpose. A story is also useful in that it passes an experience from one human to another. Stories are not advice. They share an experience that the listener can personalize if he wishes.

## SIMPLE MACHINE UNIT: TENTH GRADERS' FIRST QUARTER

If the simple machine unit were for the tenth graders' first quarter, the teacher would need to point out the need for a problem-noticing and problem-solving process from the tenth-grader perspective. The example might involve dating, learning how to drive, peer pressure, or drinking or drugs, depending upon the problems he has seen his students struggling with at that specific time. The teacher needs to pick a story that would build the need for a problem-noticing and problem-solving strategy.

The stories used to point to the need for the content area purpose should be age-appropriate for that group or age of students and be concerns-oriented. This awareness of student concerns (a "with-it-ness" skill) demonstrates the teacher truly understands and cares about making the material to be learned relevant to the needs of the students. This relationship orientation plays a pivotal role in designing a classroom where the teacher and students work together in learning.

The concerns orientation also sets the stage for the use of humor in the classroom. Things that stress us as humans may cause us to do one of two things: laugh or cry. The ability to recognize stressors in our students' lives allows the teacher the opportunity to help relieve some of the stress by pointing out the humorous or stress-relieving sides of the issue. Laughing about a stressful situation helps relieve some of the stress of the situation and opens the topic for further conversation.

The teacher must also understand the difference between finding humor in a situation versus making fun of the individual. Also in the public school setting, sarcasm never works. It is too sophisticated a technique for the age of the students and should never be used, period.

Selecting a story about dating issues yields a full measure of humorous situations that both points out the need for a problem-noticing and problem-solving process and connects the students to other humans who have experienced the same types of emotions and situations. It is a topic that is age-appropriate and with which they are engaged. Saying the wrong thing, speaking the wrong words, picking the wrong time, and misunderstandings between two people all are grist for the humor mill.

Finding one story that would meet the concerns orientation criteria for an entire class is unrealistic because each class is made up of individuals with individual needs. Over the course of the unit, semester, or school year, it is important to select stories that are as different as possible. Different genders, different viewpoints, and different interests are balanced by the awareness of stereotyping.

The focus of step 1 is to convince the students that what they are being asked to learn is directly related to their lives today. The content area purpose is worthy, relevant, and meaningful to each individual.

## STEP 2

Share how working toward the content area purpose will enhance their quality of life. In order to talk about enhancing the quality of student lives, the teacher has to passionately believe in the importance of the content area purpose. He has to passionately see that his content area helps each and every student learn to his potential. Learning with a purpose does make a difference.

Understanding yourself and others makes a difference. Communicating effectively makes a difference. Noticing and describing patterns makes a difference. Making decisions based on appropriate criteria makes a difference. Noticing and solving problems makes a difference. Applying learning to new situations makes a difference. Adapting to new contexts makes a difference.

What you teach has to make a difference in the quality of life of the student, or maybe it does not need to be taught. Life is not about *Jeopardy* and not about trivia. It is about living lives that make a difference.

Step 2 asks that the teacher make this explicit to the learners. He needs to tell the students how it all works together, how all the pieces of their learning come together into one cohesive whole. He needs to communicate effectively how the learning will make a difference in their lives today and then in a changing future. Passionate belief in the power of learning is the essence of step 2.

## SIMPLE MACHINE UNIT: TENTH GRADERS' FIRST QUARTER

Students have problems. Everyone has problems. Where do they learn how to systematically identify and solve those problems? From their friends? Through luck? Through trial and error? Is there nowhere in schools where they can learn how to do this task explicitly?

In science class, that's where! That's where we learn the steps, logic, skills, and techniques by which we deal with life's issues. We practice those life skills in the safety of science experiments. We identify, clarify, design, experiment, and learn how to notice and solve the problems of our lives. Science content allows us to practice something important, owning our lives!

Students need to know that what they are learning is important. They need to know that their learning will make a difference in their changing world. They want adults and mentors to convince them that their learning is the most important thing that is going on and they are passionately committed to making it happen. They need to hear that we care.

## STEP 3

Share the learning vision that is aligned with the purpose. Step 3 involves using content and curriculum in such a way as to meet both the curriculum goals as established along with the needs of the students. Step 3 asks the teacher to introduce the relevant essential questions for the unit of instruction.

Relevant essential questions (Kolis 2009) ask the teacher to understand the needs of his students at that place and time. They also ask the teacher to understand his content so deeply that he can connect student learning to the central concepts (enduring ideas) (Wiggins and McTighe 1998) of his field. Relevant essential questions focus on student needs while using content as the mechanism to achieve the learning goal.

Curriculum says this specific material must be taught, covered, or learned, so the teacher must look at the curriculum very deeply in order to uncover the theme or deep pattern within the minutia. He must look deeper in the curriculum to find what is worthy of a vision, for the vision must be a measurable outcome that the students will find worth striving toward.

The learning vision must be performance-oriented (the more real the audience, the better), be viewed as fun (appropriately challenging) by the students, and, in the best case, provide opportunities for individual or small group choice with the same end in mind.


## SIMPLE MACHINE UNIT: TENTH GRADERS' FIRST QUARTER

The science curriculum might point out the need to cover each type of simple machine and calculate forces and mechanical advantage, both real and ideal. The teacher would need to study the curriculum more deeply and realize that what he must really teach is problem-noticing and problem-solving. Then he must look for a vision that would allow the students to learn both about simple machines while practicing their problem-noticing and problem-solving skills in a way that was measurable and meaningful to the students.

A relevant essential question might be like one of the following: How do I get the most of my effort? What does work mean? Why are machines my friends?

The vision for learning, stated as the relevant essential question, must make the case for the learner that the purpose will be addressed by doing this particular learning experience. It must be measurable, directly aligned with the purpose, and derived from the study of the curriculum.


## STEP 4

Address the goals and objectives. Mark out the path(s), and speak to the trees issues. Step 4 is the most specific step in terms of details of the learning task at hand. It speaks to the who, what, when, and where of the journey. In other words, step 4 outlines the path through the forest and the trees that mark out the path. It attempts to provide more concrete reasons for working toward the vision and purpose, reasons more extrinsic in nature.

Step 4 addresses issues such as the specific skills that will be addressed as functions of the larger picture, as well as specific checkpoints for the journey. The sequence of tasks at hand include expectations, choices students will make, assessments, and audience issues. Mini-celebrations and learner successes are the focal point for these learning points and help guide both teacher and learners along the way.

Choices are also emphasized with the end in mind (Covey, 1998; Wiggins and McTighe, 1998). Students are informed to the options they have to demonstrate they have achieved the vision. Choice one, two, or three (multiple intelligence variety) or "see me" allows a framework for choice and an open-endedness option for those who wish. Choice might also involve the social interaction options of alone or small group work, again with the end in mind.

Even more specific information must also be provided in terms of grades and assessments for those who are motivated by those factors. This includes the percent of the final grade the project will constitute and how will the points be earned and distributed. Time frames are also included so students know what the entire process will constitute.

Last, final assessment issues are touched upon, with more detail provided later in the unit. Criteria for assessment are identified at a surface level. Finally sharing who will be invited to the final performance and assessment, the audience, is made clear. The more real the audience, parents, and community, the more meaningful the learning experience.

## SIMPLE MACHINE UNIT: TENTH GRADERS' FIRST QUARTER

Students will spend three days learning and experiencing all the types of simple machines, research complex machines online and in the library, and design the machine they wish to build. They may pick any two or more simple machines to include. They will have the following choices: power or effort category. They may work in groups of twos or threes or see me for special circumstances.

This unit will be worth half of their quarter grade with checkpoints worth half the total points. The final project is worth half the total points. Parents will be invited to attend the final performance, which will take place from 7:00 to 7:45 PM on a Thursday evening five weeks from now. A mechanical engineer from town will be the final assessor, along with the teacher.

The total time for the unit will be eight weeks.

## COMPELLING WHY EXAMPLE: SIMPLE MACHINE UNIT: TENTH GRADERS' FIRST QUARTER

### Step 1: Pick and Tell a Story from Student's Perspective

Good morning, ladies and gentlemen. To begin class today, I would like to share an experience I had yesterday. As you all know, I spend much of my time between classes monitoring the hallway. As I was standing there leaning against my door yesterday, I noticed some new types of behaviors. I saw girls I had never seen in this hallway and lots of young men strutting and preening around each other, especially when the new girls walked by. There were also groups of students standing around talking very intensely about something that was clearly important to them.

Being an adult and therefore invisible to many of the students, I had the opportunity to overhear, against my will, what a particular group of young men were talking about. It seems they were interested in getting their first homecoming date. They were asking each other who this particular young lady was, who they thought the other guys thought they should ask, or what a particular girl would say if asked. They were clearly anxious, nervous, and, at the same time, excited about the prospect of getting a date to homecoming and being on their first big date, especially because they were going to be driving themselves.

It was especially interesting in that two of the guys seemed to already have dates. They were telling the other guys about their experiences in asking girls out. What was especially interesting was how different all the guys were. There were some big guys and some guys who were already shaving. Then some guys were about ninety-five pounds. It was as if one way of asking a girl to the dance would work for all of them!

As I was listening, I got to thinking about their experiences with dating. Being the science teacher I am, I connected it to why we study science. As we have already mentioned this year, science is all about problem-noticing and problem-solving. Getting a date to homecoming is what we might define as a problem. It's not a bad problem. It's just a problem.

### Step 2: Tell How Problem-Noticing and Problem-Solving Might Enhance the Quality of Their Lives

Problems are part of everyone's daily lives, like problems getting dates, getting the grades you want, and understanding the difference between what you want and what you need and a million others. There are, of course, multiple ways to go about solving your problems. You might listen to a friend, do what your parents tell you to do (ha ha), go online and do a search to see what other people have done, or just flip a coin.

The cool thing about doing science is that we get to practice noticing, defining, and then solving problems. All the steps we learn in here are exactly the steps you could use to solve your own problems in your daily lives outside the classroom. That is powerful stuff.

Every single one of us needs to be in control of our own lives, and that means owning and solving your own problems. It means asking your own questions, finding your own information, and planning to do something to deal with the problem you have identified. Science helps you understand your own power and can give you more personal freedom.

### Step 3: Share the Learning Vision That Is Aligned with the Content Area Purpose

To that end and to help you learn the science content I am supposed to be teaching you, we will be beginning our next unit of study. We will be practicing being scientists while investigating the following relevant essential question. How do I get the most of my effort?

### Step 4: Share the Goals and Objectives along the Learning Journey

We will be practicing all the steps of the scientific method that we have learned while looking at all types of simple machines. At the end of the unit, you will be building your own machine that will lift one gallon of water two feet into the air. You will get to pick the category for your machine, work or power, as well as deciding whether to work in a group of my choice or individually. You will have to pick before I tell you your group.

This unit will be worth approximately 75 percent of your quarter grade, which includes homework and daily tasks, as well as your final write-up and formal presentation. You will be making a DVD of what you have learned about the relevant essential question. Rubrics will be explained later. I will be inviting all your parents and guardians to attend an open house where your DVDs will be presented. This is deep stuff, so this unit will be lasting for the next eight weeks.

## Chapter 19

# Compelling Whys as Beginning Points

While telling a good Compelling Why is important and sets the tone for the learning experiences, nothing is as powerful as what is actually being modeled. What you do is incredibly more powerful than what you say. Congruence may be defined as "walking the talk," where your actions and your words are both saying the same thing.

If the talk (Compelling Why) deals with visions, choices, and working toward goals and objectives, then the walk (lesson and unit plans) is the fulfillment of that language. In the case of the Compelling Why, it may therefore change virtually everything, depending upon current classroom practices.

Lesson plans demonstrate teaching and learning knowledge on the part of the teacher. Learning activities are the concrete manifestations of the purpose and vision for learning that the teacher and students have. Learning activities require the teacher to exhibit all three types of knowledge. The trees within the forest represent content knowledge.

Each tree represents an individual skill to be learned within the big, deep pattern of the content area. The path represents the knowledge of the learning process. Learning activities are organized in such a way that long-term student learning actually takes place. The knowledge of the learners is represented by the end in mind, the purpose driving the vision. Time frames, abilities and ability levels, needs, previous experiences, and skills all play a role in determining where each student is currently on the learning continuum in relationship to where they need to go in order to be successful people.

Learning activities that manifest all three types of knowledge are tied to purpose and vision, every day and in every learning activity. There is direct alignment between each skill to be learned and the end toward which the teacher and students are working.

The skills and tools that are to be learned are the same no matter which choice is selected while levels of complexity vary among the choices. This variety is a fun issue (educationally defined as "appropriately challenging"), hoping "every student will find a choice that is intrinsically interesting."

One example of having one goal with choice is that, while everyone might have to do research (the skill), he may use different sources to demonstrate that ability. Some might use World Book encyclopedias; others might use Britannica. Some might use a videotape; others might use an audiotape. Yet others will use an interview with an acknowledged expert within the field. Readability issues, interest issues, learning strength, and weakness issues are thereby addressed while the skill itself is not diminished.

Lowering the learning standard sends the message that the teacher has little or no faith in the learner. Choices in how that standard is to be met send the message that individual strengths and weaknesses do matter, as long as the end is achieved and learned. Learning activities must be designed so different paths to the same end exist (Tomlinson 2001).

Each skill along the learning path must be deemed crucial in and of itself as well as the foundation to success for the next skill. Each skill must work together synergistically to the success of the whole if the students are to see them as important enough to change their behaviors. Each skill must be so crucial that the learner can't do the final thing right if he has not done each piece correctly. Students must see the interconnectedness of the skills within the whole.

Teachable moments need to be built into the learning activities in such a way that the teacher knows, beyond a shadow of a doubt, that each student or group of students will ask this specific question sometime during the course of the activity. The teacher must also hold himself in check so he does not attempt to answer the question before the students ask it. He cannot save the students. He must exhibit the patience and perseverance to let the learning process take place.

Teachers must also build in social, emotional, and intellectual support within the learning unit. Parents, other students, other adults, and experts must be identified and utilized in such a way as to enhance student learning. The parent role must be modified to that modeled by kindergarten and first grade, emotional support and mentorship rather than surrogate teacher.

When required, teachers must also provide skills-based training for the people providing support. Support people must be taught to provide help and support, not answers. Everyone is an expert about something. The teacher's trick is to find out what it is and then use that expertise to enhance the learning of the students.

Another part of the teacher's lesson planning needs to include communication to and with parents. The teacher must convince the parents that he cares about each individual student as much as the parent does. He must convince the parent that what he is asking the students to learn is crucial to their future success. He must provide a Compelling Why for the parents as well as for the students. With the end in mind, the teacher can transform the role of parent from surrogate teacher to one of emotional support and mentorship for student for the child.

Learning activities must also be organized and structured to be checkpoint-oriented. These checkpoints serve as markers along the learning path and must be organized into some sort of learning sequence as well. The checkpoints for learning must be reached, although alternative routes are certainly acceptable. Each checkpoint must be considered crucial by both the teacher and the students, for, if can be skipped, then how important was it? Each and every checkpoint marks a spot along the learning path, and each is structured with the end in mind.

Practice opportunities must also be built into the learning activities. It takes time to acquire new patterns of behavior and thought. It takes time, effort, and practice with concentration. One step back and two steps forward exemplifies the learning process that must occur before the new pattern is internalized. Practice does not make perfect. Practice makes permanent. Only perfect practice makes perfect.

Sending students home to practice a skill where the pattern is still new virtually guarantees that the teacher will have to reteach that skill, spending time unlearning imperfect patterns. A general rule of thumb is to not have students practice a skill independently until you are reasonably certain they can do the skill successful. Otherwise, the pattern stands a high probability of being mis-learned. Relearning a skill takes even more time than doing it right the first time.

A healthy way of viewing student performance is with a redo mentality. Redo means that the skill has not been learned to the standard required, so the student may or must redo the task. A redo is not a punishment. They represent a natural consequence of learning.

If a person wanted to learn how to do a 180 on a skateboard, doing a 150 would not be viewed as a success. Most likely, the person would continue practicing until the goal was met, a 180. Doing a 160 would tell the student how far along he had come and inform him of how much farther he had to go.

A redo tells the students that the learning is so important that they cannot continue along the learning path until the individual skill has been mastered at a developmentally appropriate level.

Finally, the entire learning unit must be designed from the ending task forward, backwards planning (Wiggins and McTighe 1998). The teacher must have a clear idea of how the learning is going to be assessed before he begins any planning at all. He must know what the final project is going to entail and how it will be assessed before individual learning activities are begun.

Learning activities represent the trees and the path for the learning unit (the skills, goals, and objectives), but they must absolutely be aligned with the end in mind, the vision that gives all the learning a context and purpose.

Finally, learning projects also need to be complex and interesting, and students are preferably offered a choice list with a "see me" option. The following list is only the beginning. There are literally hundreds if not thousands of other choices available as well.

| | | |
|---|---|---|
| Concerts | Play | Presentations |
| Poetry slams | Story hours | Wax museums |
| Demonstrations | Dinners | Contests (against standards) |
| Games | Open houses | Beach parties |
| Businesses | Improv | Video productions |
| Dramas | Yearbooks | Model United Nations |
| Experiments | Reenactments | Dioramas |
| Models | Songs | Music |
| Picture albums of the journey | Art shows | Computer simulations |

What is crucial to the success of any project is that students have choice and ownership. That means they must both design and perform the task if it is to be meaningful.

Assessment strategies (Stiggins 1997) for a comprehensive learning unit require an assessment plan including a little of this (informal and formative) and a little of bit of that (formal and summative). The teacher needs to plan some quizzes and tests for content assessment and some checkpoints for information about where the students are on the learning path. Some assessments need to be group-focused while individual assessments play the largest role. Performance assessments are the largest portion of the assessment strategy and need to be criteria-based with effective rubrics. No matter how the individual assessments take place, in every single case, they need to be structured with the vision in mind.

Once the learning journey is begun, the teacher must use and call upon the content area purpose and relevant essential question every day. He must say the words (content area purpose) on a daily basis and align every learning activity to the relevant essential question. The teacher's role is literally to be the "keeper of the vision."

Their passion must emanate from the belief that the learning journey at hand is a quality-of-life issue for the students. It's not about grades. It's not about passing. It's not about school curriculum or getting higher scores on the national test. It's about students learning something that is crucial to their success as human beings. What is to be learned is relevant and meaningful to the students today and provides a foundation for the learning tomorrow.

It is also crucial that the teacher keep the vision himself. Once a vision has been established, only two choices exist: move toward your vision or forget your vision and do what you have always done. The teacher must have the intestinal fortitude and support to persevere when things do not go as planned.

The teacher must view the journey toward the vision as a creative task (Davis 2004), always looking for other ways when stuck on a strategy that is not working. He must never give up, for he must have the belief that some-day, something he might say, will be exactly the right thing at the right time for that individual learner. He must exhibit an overabundance of hope and confidence in each and every learner and show it, because if he doesn't, how will the learner ever succeed as a human being?

The teacher must also take advantage of the teachable moments as they emerge, even when it disrupts what he had originally planned. Teachable moments are the short track to long-term learning and may be viewed as the ultimate effective lesson plan.

For those teachable moments that have been designed into lesson plans and emerge as if spontaneous, the teacher, no matter how tired nor how many times he has already answered the question, must take advantage of the learning opportunity with enthusiasm and joy. The teacher cannot save himself time or effort by answering the student question beforehand. He must wait until each student or group asks and then answer it right then. Learning dictates a just-enough-at-the-right-time mentality.

The teacher must also seek to promote independence and interdependence among the learners. Giving students too much help, helping too soon, or pro-viding too much help too soon communicates little confidence in the learner. When teachers continually save their students from struggle, they ultimately enable them.

The teacher must learn to use encouragement for emotional support, feed-forward (via hints, cues, clues, and information) for both the learning right now and next time for task success, and task-specific approval so the learner knows what's right about the task. The teacher must understand the differ-ence between what the student wants and needs and be able to view that difference with the end in mind.

The teacher must also monitor the checkpoints for learning everyday. He must develop a skill termed as "professional nagging," which provides a safety net for the learners. Professional nagging is a skill that, when utilized correctly, makes it easier for the student to do the task and then face the teacher day after day explaining why the task has not been completed.

Professional nagging reduces the risk of learning and allows the student to save face because he wasn't really interested in the learning. He just wanted to get the teacher off his back! Professional nagging is also another teacher perseverance issue for it is always easier to ignore those who are not doing their tasks rather than talk to them on a daily basis.

If the teacher and the students are on a learning journey together, then the teacher must also exhibit the fact that he is learning along with the students. The teacher must model effective learning. He needs to be the best learner in the classroom. If he is, then he also needs to explain his own learning process while it is taking place.

The learning teacher needs to speak of his own frustrations, his own successes, and his own strategies in order to model for his students what learning is all about. This helps the teacher convince the students that the classroom is, in fact, a learning classroom for everyone. "We are in this together" becomes the reality.

The teacher need not worry about knowing all the answers himself. What he needs is to have confidence in his ability to learn and look for help and experts. He needs to involve others in providing help for student learning, realizing that connecting students to other adults and experts enhances everyone's lives, not just the student's.

Finally, the teacher must celebrate the learning of each individual and the group. Celebrations of learning should never be held hostage by the individual or the few who have struggled with the learning process. Celebrations of learning are also not rewards—"If you do this, then we …" (Kohn 1993). They are unconditional. Celebrations are times to review the struggle, successes, frustrations, and misadventures and are organized to commemorate the time and effort that the learning has required.

Celebrations of learning provide opportunities to exhibit a true community of learners. Everyone has the opportunity to be front and center at some time during the performance and celebration, and each individual's success does not detract from the success of anyone else. Everyone gets to shine.

It's like in the musical, *The Music Man*. Harold Hill sells bands to boys, but really just swindles the people out of their money because he doesn't really know anything about teaching music. His teaching method involves a progressive new technique that he has termed "thinkology" where the student doesn't actually practice their instrument. They just "think" the music. When he is finally caught and the band must actually perform, the band is terrible. He is worried about being tarred and feathered and run out of the county … until one mother stands up and shouts, "That's my boy!" That's what celebrations need to be about!

# Section 4

# Conclusion

"When placed in the same system, people, however different, tend to produce similar results" (Senge 42). In other words, the systemic structure of a system produces similar, specific types of behaviors among different individuals. The current model of schooling with its emphasis upon sorting rather than learning produces consistent behaviors within and among teachers, administrators, students, classrooms, schools, and their interactions with parents and their communities.

Schooling in the United States is a system. It's not good or bad. It just is. To be unaware of that system, your role within it, how it works, how the pieces interact, and how it causes certain types of behaviors is to be held prisoner by its current structure.

Interestingly, systems do not learn. Only people learn. What individuals within the system learn (not memorize) determines if and how the system itself will change. Doing things as they have always been done virtually guarantees that the system will remain unchanged.

Systems can be changed, but not by working harder with less, quick fixes, consultants, nor simplistic, stopgap measures. Leverage (the idea of using your energies in such as way as to change the system itself) is the key point. Leverage means focusing your individual efforts and learning where it will do the most good in such a way that the system itself will not revert to its original form when your individual efforts cease.

There are many examples of extraordinary schools in the United States, but, when key individuals leave, the school almost always reverts back to its former structure. This reverting-to-the-norm behavior is an indication that the system itself had not changed, but was only influenced by powerful, caring, purpose-driven individuals.

Schools are filled with many competent, highly trained, caring, and dedicated professionals caught in a system of which they are unaware and which influences their behaviors. A powerful lever exists to change the system, and that is to agree upon the purpose of schooling and the purposes of the content areas.

When a clear and powerful purpose is explicitly named and used as the criteria for making all daily choices, the system can be changed to benefit more students. This new structure might in fact be more consistent with our deepest hopes and dreams for each and every student.

Purpose acts as the foundation for visions. A true vision provides the impetus for changes in behaviors. To agree upon purpose is to agree at the very deepest level of understanding and acts as the basis for a powerful and shared commitment to long-term growth and change.

Content area purposes are the individual facets of the schooling lens within the classroom and content courses. Each content area exists for a specific purpose. Together, they help individual students begin their journey toward becoming self-actualized citizens.

Personal growth includes individual learning and new and/or modified knowledge. Skills are required. Knowledge of students, content, and how people learn must continually be revised, reviewed, and reflected upon. Skills must be developed and honed if students are to learn rather than memorize. Adults in the schools must be the very best learners and act and model learning every single day for their students.

Change is tough stuff. It includes risk, failures, redos, reflection, trial and error, and perseverance to hold the vision when the outlook is bleak. It is also deeply and powerfully empowering to the individual. Only individuals can learn, and they will only learn what they think is worth their time, effort, and resources. We can make some people memorize some things (if they want the grade), but learning is always individual. To make schooling relevant and meaningful to every student is the lever to changing school structures.

# References

Covey, SR. *The Seven Habits of Highly Effective People*. New York: Simon & Schuster, 1989.

Darling-Hammond et al. *Powerful Learning*. San Francisco: Jossey-Bass, 2008.

Davis, GA. *Creativity is Forever*, 5th ed. Dubuque: Kendall/Hunt, 2004.

Diamond, M. and J. Hopson. *Magic Trees of the Mind*. New York: Dutton, 1998.

Gardner, H. *Frames of Mind*. New York: Basic Books, 1983.

Glasser, W. *Choice Theory in the Classroom*. New York: HarperPerennial, 2001.

Hart, LA. *Human Brain and Human Learning*. New York and London: Longman, 1983.

Jensen, E. *Teaching with the Brain in Mind*. Alexandria, Va.: ASCD, 1998.

Kohn, A. *Punished by Rewards*. Boston: Houghton Mifflin, 1993.

Kolis, MW. "Making Essential Questions Relevant." *Silhouettes* 120 (2009). www. national@atriskeducation.ccsend.com.

Kotulak, R. *Inside the Brain*. Kansas City: Andrews McMeel Publishing, 1997.

Maslow, AH. *Toward a Psychology of Being*, 3rd ed. New York: John Wiley & Sons, 1999.

Oakes, J. *Keeping Track*, 2nd ed. New York and London: Yale University Press, 2005.

Senge, PM. *The Fifth Discipline*. New York: Currency Doubleday, 1990.

Sousa, DA. *How the Brain Learns*, 2nd ed. Thousand Oaks, Calif.: Corwin Press, Inc., 2001.

Stiggins, RJ. *Student-Centered Classroom Assessment*, 2nd ed. Upper Saddle River, N.J.: Merrill, 1997.

Sylwester, R. *A Celebration of Neurons*. Alexandria, Va.: ASCD, 1995.

Tomlinson, CA. *How to Differentiate Instruction in Mixed Ability Classrooms*, 2nd ed. Alexandria, Va.: ASCD, 2001.

Wiggins, G. and J. McTighe. *Understanding by Design*. Alexandria, Va.: ASCD, 1998.

# Index

# About the Author

**Mickey Kolis**, recently awarded the University of Wisconsin–Eau Claire "Excellence in Teaching" award, team-teaches with four university faculty every day with student cohorts. He is working collaboratively to help beginning educators change the system, one person at a time.